Plans for Better Behaviour in the Primary School

Management and Intervention

Sue Roffey and Terry O'Reirdan

JAY

David Fulton Publishers

London

David Fulton Publishers Ltd
The Chiswick Centre, 414 Chiswick High Road, London W4 5TF
www.fultonpublishers.co.uk

David Fulton Publishers is a division of Granada Learning Ltd, part of the
Granada Media group.

First published 2003
10 9 8 7 6 5 4 3 2 1

British Library Cataloguing in Publication Data
A catalogue record for this book is available from the British Library.

ISBN 1 85346 971 8

Typeset by Servis Filmsetting Ltd, Manchester
Printed and bound in Great Britain by Thanet Press Limited, Margate, Kent

Contents

Preface

Plans for Better Behaviour in the Primary School is based on Haringey's Behaviour Guidelines for Primary Schools, written and produced by and for the London Borough of Haringey. These Guidelines were cited as good practice by the Department for Education (DfEE circular 1/98). Sue coordinated the working group which put the Guidelines together and Terry, at the time coordinator of the borough's Behaviour Support Team, was a key contributor. The format used is based on the categories for behavioural difficulties which can be found in the authors' earlier book, *Young Children and Classroom Behaviour*.

The suggestions here are those which teachers have used and found helpful in their classrooms. They have arisen from an eclectic mix of educational and psychological research and theory. These include social learning theory, behavioural and cognitive behavioural psychology, Vygotsky's learning theories, Glasser's choice theory, personal and social constructs, ecosystemic, interactive perspectives and solution focused thinking. There is also an emphasis on emotional intelligence at various levels. Although theoretical underpinnings are not overtly spelt out, this book illustrates how these theories translate into practice. Behavioural intervention is frequently useful for immediate management strategies but other approaches are often required to achieve longer-term change. Although the content here is largely about management and intervention for individual children we do not advocate a 'medical' model of behavioural difficulties where problems are seen to reside only within individuals who therefore need to be 'labelled' and 'treated'. This is not seen as useful or effective within an educational setting and a range of interactive, contextual factors in establishing and maintaining appropriate school behaviour is acknowledged throughout.

Many of the issues raised here are potentially complex and for some, such as bullying, much research has been carried out and many books have been written. The ideas for management and intervention in this book are intended to be those that busy educators can easily access and use and on which they might build. We recommend further reading on many of the issues and strategies covered and have given details of relevant literature in the references section.

It is not only *what* is carried out which is important but also *how* these suggestions are put into place. Never underestimate the effects that consistent small changes in approaches and language may have.

NB: When teachers are mentioned here this includes all those adults who are working within the educational setting, including classroom assistants and learning mentors. Likewise when we refer to parents this incorporates all those who have a care responsibility for the child. We have used the words: child, student and pupil interchangeably and alternated the gender of individuals.

Acknowledgements

The members of the working group who put the original guidelines together included teachers, psychologists, behaviour support teachers and special needs coordinators. We would like to acknowledge their contribution to this final product. Special thanks go to Sue Freeman, Juliet Goldstone, Maura Steggal, Rachel Tester-Robson, Mollie Bird, Chris Sey and Suzanne Carmichael. Pupils at Lordship Lane and Earlsmead Primary Schools provided the illustrations. We also thank the London Borough of Haringey for their support and for giving us permission to use the original material as a basis for this publication.

Much of the work for this project relied on collaboration from opposite ends of the world, Terry in London and Sue in Sydney. It was all made possible by the wonders of information technology. Dominic O'Reirdan and David Roffey came to the rescue every time the quirks of cyberspace left us frustrated and floundering. We are grateful to them both for their expertise and ready willingness to help out.

Dedication

This book is dedicated to all those in education who, despite the overwhelming demands and pressures of the job, remain motivated by the desire to make a positive difference for children.

Part One: Introduction

Plans for Better Behaviour in the Primary School provides a selection of ideas to help teachers and others manage and respond to a variety of behaviours which impact on learning in the primary classroom. The book is intended as a handy reference for educators to dip into as the need arises.

Although the plans and strategies outlined here give guidance about managing incidents of difficult behaviour it is important to remember that behaviour management is most effective when

- it is consistent with whole-school policy and practice which promotes positive behaviour;
- a positive relationship between the adult and the child concerned has been established so that the child feels that he matters;
- parents are involved as closely as possible in a way that they feel valued;
- the child's sense of self-worth and self-efficacy is developed and maintained;
- teachers feel supported in their endeavours and are able to retain professional integrity.

Behaviour is the outcome of many interactive factors, some of which are more open to change than others. What adults do and don't do can have a powerful impact on the way children's behaviour changes over time. Teachers and other adults in school can have significant influence on the following:

- teaching styles and approaches;
- classroom layout and use of resources;
- expectations of children and the demands placed upon them;
- classroom atmosphere and ethos;
- how children think and feel about themselves;
- ensuring that children have structured opportunities to experience success;
- the way parents and carers are valued in the school context;
- school policy and practice for behaviour management;
- the discourse in school about children who present with difficulties and their families;
- how staff support each other.

It is easy to become discouraged when progress in improving behaviour appears slow or minimal. Consistent good practice takes determination and patience. Teachers need to feel that their efforts are acknowledged and supported. This can be done by a joint celebration of progress, however small. Share successes with children, colleagues and with parents. An emphasis on targets, achievements, solutions, strengths and competencies is more effective and motivating than simply focusing on problems and deficits.

Using this book

Which behaviour?

Children who are struggling often manifest difficult behaviour in a variety of ways and in a variety of situations. Adults sometimes find it difficult to know which problem behaviours to address first. Should it be the area that appears to causing most difficulty for the student or perhaps what is most problematic for the teacher? Should it be an underlying behaviour that is affecting other things? Children who do not easily settle to work, for instance, may also be disruptive so it might be best to work on strategies to help the child to settle first rather than attempt to deal with the disruptions. Although it is tempting to begin with the most entrenched difficulty it is often more productive to attempt to change the behaviour which is more likely to respond to intervention first. When the student begins to feel more effective and successful in school as a result of interventions put in place to address less serious concerns, behaviour often improves overall as the spiral of negativity begins to be replaced with a spiral of success.

Although children often display difficulties in many areas, for ease and speed of access to plans and ideas, behavioural issues have been arranged in five chapters.

Part Two: Settling to work

This is where a child may not appear to focus on instructions or follow directions. The student may flit from activity to activity, completing very little. She may show little motivation to achieve and may be restless and impulsive.

Part Three: General disruptive behaviour

This applies to the child who seeks attention inappropriately, responds badly to limits being set, may want to please but in the process annoys/distracts others. This behaviour is wearing and while an individual incident may not appear to be significant, the frequency and duration of such incidents can be a major source of stress for adults.

Part Four: Social interactions

This applies to the child who has difficulty in establishing and maintaining friendships. Bullying behaviour, difficulties in the playground and poor group skills would fit into this category.

Part Five: Emotional distress

This section is intended to give guidance to teachers in dealing with children who are generally hostile, have poor self-control, who may have very negative views of themselves and others and/or are clearly distressed in some way.

Part Six: Unusual behaviours

Some children behave in ways which may puzzle and even alarm the adults who witness their behaviour. This final section covers behaviours which fall into this category and gives some guidance on actions to take for management and intervention in the short term before more specialised advice is given. Child protection procedures should, however, always be followed if behaviour is indicative of such a concern.

Each section has a brief introduction followed by individual pages detailing behaviours that may fall into this category. It is not intended to cover every behaviour. Those which have been included either occur most commonly in schools or cause teachers most concern.

Each page is divided into columns. The first column names the behaviour that is problematic and identifies a related target behaviour to aim for. Prerequisite learning may also be included. The second column gives some ideas for assessment. The third column suggests short-term management strategies while the fourth outlines possible intervention plans for longer-term change.

Assessment

We may not be able to do much about the causes of unwanted behaviour but we can do something about what is happening now. In order to do this, it is essential to formulate some idea of what is maintaining or, indeed, modifying the behaviour. Meeting with families would normally be part of the process of gaining additional information which may be useful. As well as finding out about any concerns they may have, parents will be able to give their perspective and also valuable information. This could, for example, be about the student's language skills, general levels of maturity and events at home which might be contributing to his difficulties in school. Assessment also needs to look at the child's strengths, how he may view the situation and what would be helpful to him. Finding out what is happening in the playground and/or classroom, such as interactions and expectations, may also give useful clues to intervention. It is often helpful for an assessment to include establishing a baseline against which improvements can be measured. The following explains the terms used in the assessment column:

Context: In which contexts does this behaviour occur – in the classroom, in the playground, at home, everywhere, or in specific situations only?

Frequency: How often does this behaviour occur? This may be estimated using a tally.

Tally: This simply means keeping count of every time a particular behaviour is observed during a particular time-frame, e.g. during a half-hour. It will sometimes involve using an adult as observer.

Duration: For some behaviours it is how long the child 'keeps it up' that is important. It is important that this is accurately determined as those experiencing the effects of difficult behaviour may overestimate its duration.

Patterns: Is there a pattern to the behaviour? Is it more frequent at certain times of the week, of the day, after, before or during certain activities?

ABC: This stands for antecedent, behaviour and consequence. Using an ABC framework, consideration is given to what is happening for the student concerned immediately before and immediately after a particular behaviour. This involves observation carried out over a particular and usually short time-frame. With this knowledge it is sometimes possible to alter the immediate antecedents and therefore prevent the behaviour from occurring in the first place. It may be possible to change the consequences, e.g. not giving attention for negative behaviour so that the frequency of the behaviour diminishes.

Triggers: Is there something – action, event or social interaction – which triggers this behaviour?

Onset: When was the behaviour first seen? What is known about the child's life at that time which may help to explain this behaviour? Has there been a distinct change recently or has an established behaviour intensified?

Perception: What are the child's constructs, what sense is she making of her own behaviour? How does she think it might be meeting her needs? Do negative thoughts underpin the child's responses in certain situations? What might be open to change?

Ability: What evidence is there that the child is able to do what he is being asked to do? What is the difference between what he is able to do unaided and what he is able to achieve with support? It is important to remember that a significant proportion of children who present with behaviour difficulties have another underlying unmet need, e.g., a speech and language delay/disorder.

Competencies: What does the child/family/teacher already do that may contribute towards a creative solution to a difficulty?

Establishing positive school behaviour

A critical task facing all educators whether they are teachers, classroom assistants or learning mentors is to manage the behaviour of the children they teach. They need to do so in order to establish and maintain an environment conducive to learning, both in terms of the curriculum and of social learning. This means finding ways to increase the frequency and duration of the behaviours that favour such an environment, e.g. listening to instructions, sharing equipment and attention, taking turns, working cooperatively, etc. and reducing those behaviours that interfere with meaningful teaching and learning, e.g. shouting out, non-compliance, disrupting others' work, physical aggression, etc.

Children learn about behaviour in much the same way as they learn everything else, by trying things out to see what happens, by trial and error, by watching and copying, by discovering what is rewarding and/or meets their immediate needs and by being given direct guidance. In any classroom, there will be students who appear quickly to understand and follow both formal classroom and school rules as well as the unwritten social expectations. Other pupils need more specific input. Once they have been taught ways to promote their social and emotional competencies children need opportunities to practise these new ways of interacting. If this is initially in relaxed situations where they can achieve an initial sense of heightened efficacy and self-worth, they are more likely to generalise their learning to less familiar and more challenging situations. For most children, but particularly those who are needy or emotionally distressed, the teacher–child relationship is crucial to the success of any intervention and for longer-term plans often needs to be part of the intervention.

Most of these interventions are intended for use as early intervention. Where children arrive in school with more serious or entrenched difficulties, however, these plans will help to inhibit escalation and will also provide good evidence for requesting support from external agencies if needed.

Short-term management and longer-term change

In this book, an important distinction is made between short-term management strategies and longer-term plans for better behaviour.

Imagine that you are on a motorway, travelling at above the legal speed limit, when you spot a police car up ahead. It is likely that you will slow down; at least until the police car is no longer in sight. This well placed police car provides a short-term management strategy, in that it may reduce the speed of drivers in the near vicinity for a short while. On its own, however, it is unlikely to change the behaviour of drivers in the longer term. A more intensive and longer-term programme is required to establish and internalise safer behaviour fully.

Short-term management

Routinely, in the day-to-day business of busy classrooms, adults initially take sufficient action to minimise disruption and refocus on teaching and learning. Any such action is a *short-term management strategy*.

When individuals or groups of students fail to comply with the requests of adults, or with classroom/school rules and expectations, teachers need to know what to do at that moment to manage the situation. Any intervention needs to be at a level with the degree of the misbehaviour. Low-level misbehaviours require a low-key response in the first instance, followed by stronger sanctions or consequences if needed. The opposite is also true; more serious misdemeanours, and, in particular, those where safety is compromised, may call for a higher level of response straight away.

What if nothing works?

Some behaviours, such as defiance, are potentially threatening to an adult's sense of professional competence. What is important in these cases is to maintain personal and professional integrity, even if an immediate management strategy appears to be ineffective. This means not taking the behaviour personally and acknowledging that no-one can *force* a student to behave well. If everything else fails restate expectations calmly, ensure students know what the consequences are for both compliance and non-compliance and tell them again that they have choices. Do not engage in further discussion at the time especially if it maintains the disruption or appears defensive. Pay attention to students who are responding well and acknowledge quietly any positive behaviour that the pupil exhibits. If the pupil continues with the unwanted behaviour it is essential that consequences are followed through. Later, outside of the classroom, it may be useful to acknowledge and explore the pupil's feelings and discuss how these might be expressed more constructively. Such a conversation shows an interest in the student, begins to build a relationship and may help prevent a re-occurrence.

Staying calm, clear and focused models self-respect and enables the adult to remain in charge of herself and the class. This approach also helps to maintain emotional resources for the teacher.

Primary and secondary behaviour issues

When adults interact with students about a behavioural concern, the body language or tone of voice of the student can be very irritating irrespective of whether it has been deliberately done to annoy the teacher, or to gain peer approval. This may result in conflict between pupils and teachers. The primary issue – why the adult intervened in the first instance – sometimes gets forgotten. Keeping the focus on the primary issue also keeps the adult in control.

Intervention plans for longer-term change

The majority of educators have a tried and tested range of strategies for short-term management. Although often useful for immediate resolution of a difficulty these *alone* are unlikely to bring about better behaviour in the longer term. Teachers who are frustrated may declare that they have tried everything to change the behaviour of a particular student, but it may just be that they have focused solely on short-term management without initiating longer-term plans.

Plans for longer-term change look at what a child needs in order to develop and internalise better behaviour. Such plans may be related to changes in perspective, improvements in self-esteem and self-efficacy and to systemic interventions, which involve intervention to support a child in a variety of contexts. Positive relationships are central.

Behaviour does not change overnight, and doing something once or twice is not likely to result in permanently improved behaviour. Plans need to be implemented consistently over sufficient time for interventions to prove effective. A fine balance, however, must be taken between allowing sufficient time to see change occurring and acknowledging that eventually a different approach might be needed if something does not work for a particular child.

Choosing what you do

Much of this book is about doing things differently rather than additionally. Some of the plans are intended for use with individual students while others are for groups or whole classes. It is perfectly acceptable, even desirable, for an individual programme to include other children on a regular basis, even as part of small group work, e.g. where there is the opportunity to practise skills which may have been taught on an individual basis.

Not all strategies will work with every child. What is important is the teacher's assessment of the child and situation, and the relationships that exist between adults and students. No-one should attempt to implement anything that they are not comfortable with. Although it might seem that some of the strategies are time-consuming, effort put in initially will save time and emotional resources in the long term. Choose the strategies that seem the best fit for the child, the teacher and the situation.

The underlying principles in all aspects of behaviour management are that the adults are:

- clear – rules and requests are explicit, not open to misinterpretation, and it is easily apparent when they are being complied with.
- calm – and in control of both themselves and the situation. This at times is easier said than done, and requires the adult to have developed some personal understanding about his own responses prior to intervening with pupils. Calm, however, does not mean bland. The student needs to know that the adult is aware, in control and will deal with the situation. She also needs to know that her behaviour matters to the teacher in the context of their relationship.
- consistent – where each individual adult is consistent over time in terms of his responses to students, and that practice and responses from members of the same staff team are consistent with each other.
- positive – focusing on achievements and improvements, however small.

Starred strategies

This section briefly introduces some of the ideas and strategies referred to in the text. For further details, readers are referred to the reference section at the end of this book, and in particular to the work of Jenny Mosely, Lee Canter, Bill Rogers and the authors' earlier work.

Assertiveness skills

When faced with a difficult situation there are several options: fight/be aggressive, pretend it isn't happening/do nothing or be 'appropriately assertive'. Children need to know that they have choices and that being appropriately assertive is empowering, makes them feel good and doesn't have negative consequences such as getting into trouble. This means stating clearly to the other person what you feel and what you want, using 'I' statements to do this, e.g. 'I don't like you calling me names, I want you to stop doing it.' Students are encouraged to use these statements and then walk away from the situation, possibly towards an adult or other support person.

Behaviour chart

A target behaviour is agreed with the student. Each time the pupil demonstrates this behaviour, a tick/star/sticker is placed on a chart that has been set up for her. When she has accumulated a certain number of ticks/stars, etc. then she is rewarded. The reward should also be negotiated with the student and should be within the control of the adult in school. Letters home are often welcome and can help parents focus on improvements. The younger the pupil, the more immediate should be her reward. For some children there may need to be 'interim' rewards on a daily basis. As the frequency of the behaviour increases the reward system will need to be faded out and the behaviour generalised to other settings. Though less favoured in recent years behaviour charts can be highly effective, particularly for breaking a cycle of negative behaviour. Such charts are usually used for individual pupils, and there is therefore a limit to the number of these that can be administered at any one time.

Behaviour plan

This is a simple plan/code of conduct for each area/classroom, with a few explicit rules, with details of how those rules will be reinforced (what rewards and consequences will be used). Drawing this plan up with students gives them ownership and has more chance of being effective. Students need to be regularly reminded of their behaviour plan and any compliance with it acknowledged. Some students may need to be given opportunities to practise elements of the plan.

'Broken record'

Using the 'broken-record' technique, adults do not engage in discussion with students as to why they have not complied with a reasonable request – they merely repeat the request calmly. Non-compliance is not acceptable so it is important that requests are not repeated indefinitely – if a student has not complied by the third or fourth request, a 'consequence as choice' needs to be put in place.

Circle of friends

This is a structured intervention aimed at supporting individual students who are experiencing social difficulties. Following initial liaison with parents and the child concerned and a subsequent class discussion about friendship, a small group volunteers to be the 'circle of friends'. This group then meets weekly to discuss how to support the individual concerned and help him at times of difficulty. An adult from outside the class who has had specific training usually introduces this time-limited intervention, which may then be monitored by a teacher.

Circle time activities

These are in use in many classrooms to raise self-esteem, foster group identity, support the development of emotional literacy and for problem-solving. There are basic ground rules, which need to be understood by all, and taught to pupils. Staff need to understand the underlying principles and use them appropriately. Not doing so can lead to exacerbation of difficulties in some instances.

Conditional directions

Includes such statements as 'When you have finished that piece of work, then you can go out to play,' rather than saying 'No you can't go out – you have not tidied away.' This avoids confrontations with those students who respond negatively to the word 'no'.

Conflict management

Conflict is inevitable. Individuals see things differently or want different things. It is how conflict is resolved that matters. People need to be aware of the messages they give which may exacerbate confrontation such as standing too close or pointing at someone. It is useful to check intentions rather than simply 'reading' the behaviour. Good conflict management focuses on defining priorities, establishing fairness and acknowledging feelings. The aim is to enable students to create solutions which everyone can accept, even if these are not the most desired outcomes for individuals. Models of good conflict management include being respectful, flexible and being prepared to meet others half-way.

Consequences as choice

Using consequences as a choice puts the responsibility for her behaviour on the student concerned. In some circumstances this may also allow her to 'save face'. Rather than saying, 'If you don't finish your work, I will keep you in at playtime,' this would be expressed as: 'If you choose not to finish your work now you are choosing to stay in at playtime to do it – it's up to you.' This subtle difference in language has huge implications.

Externalise problems

Talking about issues as if they were outside the child is an idea from narrative therapy. Questions could include things like: 'This problem of joining in games seems to be making you unhappy in school – what do you think might help to shrink the problem so you can have a better time?' This could also help with developing efficacy in body control, e.g. 'Your hands seem to be getting you into trouble a lot today – what can you do to keep them in order?'

Face-saving

Sometimes children paint themselves into a corner and require adult intervention to give them a way out. Some strategies for doing this might include leaving the child with an instruction and saying you will come back later to see how they have got on. Offering children a choice about when they comply or the order in which they do something or what to focus on also helps. The teacher needs to take control to calm a situation rather than allow it to become a confrontation. (See also Partial agreement.)

'I' statements

These can be very effective. Rather than saying: 'You should be working and not talking', the adult would say: 'I need you to get on with your work'; or, 'I am really unhappy when you do . . .' rather than 'You make me feel angry when you do . . .'; this subtle difference can be more acceptable to those students who are quick to assume that they are being blamed.

'The Look'

One of the simplest interventions for minor misdemeanours is eye contact between adult and student that gives the message that the adult is unhappy with what a student is doing and wishes for this to stop. There are various other 'signals' that can be similarly used. These are low-level interventions which may address the misbehaviour, while at the same time not drawing too much attention from other students. A thumbs-up signal or other expressions of approval are examples of these. The effectiveness of this strategy depends on the existence of a positive student–teacher relationship.

Marbles in the jar

This is a strategy from Assertive Discipline. It is usually used with groups of pupils. Here, the adult determines behaviour to focus on, and lets the pupils know that this is target behaviour for them, within a given time-frame. Every time this behaviour occurs, the adult places a 'marble' in a jar. When the jar is full, then the group earns a pre-agreed reward. This can be as simple as five minutes of extra playtime, or something bigger such as a non-uniform day for the class. No marbles should be removed from the jar for any misbehaviour at any time, and the time-frame for operation should be appropriate for the age and understanding of the children. Of course, the adult can manipulate the system according to the size of the jar, and of the marbles, to ensure that it is possible for the jar to be filled in the time-frame. It can be an effective strategy for changing the behaviour of a particular pupil if the adult ensures that the pupil's actions earn more marbles for the class than others. This can then increase the popularity and status of this pupil.

Mediation

Both people need to want to come to a resolution. Often a third party will help with this as in peer mediation. Each student has an agreed time to have his say without blaming the other (see Assertiveness skills and 'I' statements), then they brainstorm solutions and finally choose something they will try. (See also Problem-solving.)

Mirroring

This is a strategy for use with older pupils. Here, the adult meets with a particular student, without any other students as an audience, and both adult and student are calm. The adult first asks for permission to mirror the student's behaviour as exhibited in a recent situation, and briefly does so, perhaps saying to the student: 'This is what I observed you do.' There follows a brief discussion about possible alternative ways of dealing with the particular situation, and, if appropriate, a practice session of how the student will behave in future. The key to success is that this session is brief, that this is a strategy to teach new behaviour, and not an opportunity to reprimand or embarrass the student. For this reason, consideration needs to be given to the verbal and body language used by the adult, as well as to its timing.

Mnemonics and memory games

Mnemonics are ways of triggering memory and are popular with children. Teaching pupils to think of 'SPAR' before they start a piece of work reminds them that they need a Sharp Pencil and A Ruler. 'TOOTS' – Talking Out of Turn, is another mnemonic that teachers use. There are many more. Linking behavioural learning to what is of interest/familiar/amusing to students will enhance success.

Models

We all learn by copying what others do. It is important that the adults in schools provide an example of behaviour that is consistent with the expectations for students. Adults may deliberately model ways of handling more complex social relationship and intrapersonal skills, e.g. handling conflict, and feelings such as disappointment, anger, etc.

No-blame approach

This is one way of dealing with bullying. It concentrates on the feelings of someone who has been bullied and does not attempt to explore incidents in detail. Following discussion with the child, a group in the class, which includes those who have been bullying, are told how unhappy their classmate is. Everyone is asked to think of a way which could make this person's time in school less miserable. The teacher meets with the group weekly for about half a term to monitor this strategy and ensure the bullying has stopped.

Partial agreement

When teacher and pupil get into an argument in front of the class, many students continue or even escalate the situation rather than lose face in front of peers. In this case, it may be better to acknowledge what they have said: 'Maybe you weren't the only one who was shouting out; nevertheless, I want you to get on with your work quietly.' Or 'I know that you don't find this activity easy but I want you to have a go.'

Paula Pane

Paula Pane is an imaginary child, in a particular class, represented by a face, perhaps just eyes, ears and a mouth, drawn on a window. Rather than directing a remark/comment to a particular child in the class about her behaviour, the teacher addresses Paula. This helps 'depersonalise' perhaps more critical comments, and is a light-hearted strategy.

Permission

This is sometimes known as 'paradoxical instruction'. It entails giving children permission to do what they are already doing, e.g. 'You have a good cry and let me know when you are ready to start work again.' This strategy can be very effective as it acknowledges the emotion being expressed but also gives control back to the adult. It needs to be used with caution and only in appropriate circumstances.

Personal best

Some students feel that they can never match up to others and lose motivation. Sports commentators often refer to an athlete achieving a 'personal best' even though he did not necessarily win an event. This concept can also be applied in the classroom.

Positive feedback

Should be genuine and specific, e.g. 'I noticed the way that you two were sharing your pencils, and taking turns, well done.' Or 'You took a great deal of care with that colouring in.' Feedback to older students, or those who are uncomfortable with public praise, may have to be low-key given privately, given to a third person in the student's hearing or second-hand, e.g. 'Mr Green told me that you managed to keep very calm in that unpleasant incident in the playground yesterday, I'm really pleased.'

Positive language

When giving directions to students it is far better to use positive language when at all possible, i.e. to focus on what they should be doing, rather than what they may be doing wrong. In terms of rules, this might mean, 'Keep your hands and feet to yourself' and 'Walk in the corridor', rather than 'No hitting, pushing', etc. and 'No running in the corridor'.

Problem-solving

In some situations it increases efficacy for students to decide what to do about a difficulty. Ask them to brainstorm possibilities, choose the one they think will work best, ask if this idea needs additions or amendments to maximise the chances of success and then try it for a given period of time. Monitoring, review and positive feedback from significant adults is essential.

Proximity praise

Rather than focus on a child who is not doing what is expected, specific feedback is given to one or two who are close by and are complying. This not only gives the message of what the adult wants to the child who is not complying, it provides affirmation for those who have complied. In other words, it focuses attention on positive rather than negative behaviour.

Report cards and self-monitoring sheets

These are a development of behaviour charts, and involve the student in negotiating her own targets and regulating and recording her own behaviour. This is more suited to older students, and needs regular adult feedback.

Scripts

Many students are unable to express their wishes in ways that are acceptable without causing offence or hurting others. Some may just be at a loss as to what to say. Teaching students scripts for certain situations and role-playing those situations can develop alternative ways of responding. Some individuals may need to practise on a one-to-one basis with an adult several times before being able to transfer the skills to a real setting.

Shaping

Even if students have not completely met expectations, they may be praised for the extent to which they have met expectations, e.g. 'You have put the title and date, Jayesh, thanks, now you need to start the exercise.'

Star of the day

Each child in the class has a turn at being 'special' for a day. The 'star' is identified by a badge or similar, and has special privileges as well as responsibilities for that day. The role is a 'right', not to be used as a reward or withdrawn for misdemeanours. Used in conjunction with circle time, the 'star' can be the person in the centre of the circle, about whom other children make affirmative statements. It boosts self-esteem and encourages turn-taking and sharing attention if each child knows he will get his turn.

Symbol system

Here, a pictorial symbol or symbols (preferably meaningful for the student concerned) are used to help the student understand what is expected of her. This may mean, for example, that all the equipment that she needs for a particular activity has the same symbol on it or is of the same colour. It may also mean that a symbol/number is used to represent the order of the steps necessary to complete a particular task.

Tactical ignoring

As part of any behaviour plan, consideration will need to be given to the question of which behaviours cannot be ignored and will require immediate response from adults. *Tactical* ignoring is a planned decision not to deal with specific misbehaviours at the time they occur but at a time and location of the adult's choice. Usually the adult deals with the student when there are no other pupils to act as an audience. This is usually more effective, providing other students get the message that misdemeanours will be dealt with.

Take Two

Inappropriate behaviour is regarded as 'Take One' and as in a film shoot the director (teacher) says 'cut' and makes suggestions for improvements. The child has a chance to 'redo the scene' in 'Take Two'. It is not necessary to insist that the student follows through if this will exacerbate a situation. The message has been given. This depersonalises the behaviour, teaches more appropriate ways forward, gives pupils a second chance and can be a light-hearted approach which appeals to some children.

Take-up time

Don't stand over the child expecting him to comply immediately – sometimes this provokes defiance. Walk away, with the expectation of compliance. It is surprising how many children will comply when the pressure is off.

Time-out

Removing an individual student from the group or the classroom for a few minutes when she is being disruptive allows the rest of the group to continue and avoids the student receiving attention for negative behaviour. It is important to remember, however, that the student must receive minimal attention during the period of time-out and return to the group with minimal fuss. An opportunity to give positive, genuine feedback for appropriate behaviour shortly afterwards should be sought. Some students may be given responsibility for removing themselves from confrontations with the teacher's agreement. This fosters self-regulation and strategies for coping with difficult feelings.

Traffic lights

Most students have a concept of traffic lights. The teacher, using a cardboard replica with pointer, can indicate the noise level in the class. Green is acceptable, amber is a warning, while red indicates that the noise has reached an unacceptable level.

A variation on this idea is for students to use coloured cards. Where a student places an orange card on his desk he may need help; a red one means that he definitely needs help with a particular situation. The adult is aware that those with green cards should be managing on their own. This is one of a range of strategies that helps children begin to recognise and regulate their own emotions.

Visual cues

Some pupils experiencing receptive/expressive language difficulties may present challenging behaviour. For these pupils, as well as those with English as an additional rather than first language, visual cues used in conjunction with words can help with behaviour management as well as classroom organisation.

Ways of developing and maintaining self-esteem in the classroom

Label the behaviour as undesirable, not the child.

Use 'I' statements, e.g. 'I am finding this noise level too high' rather than 'You are being too noisy.'

Use a quiet voice when issuing a reprimand and where possible do this away from the main group.

Find an opportunity to praise the child as soon as possible after a reprimand.

Avoid making comparisons between children.

Try to give specific praise at least once a day.

Give praise for being brave enough to try.

Acknowledge the extent to which success has been achieved even if a target has not been reached.

Say something positive about the child to someone else in the child's hearing.

Offer choices wherever possible. Open-ended choices are often more difficult – limited choices may be better.

Show warmth; smile and greet children by name.

Show an interest in and remember what is important for the child and ask about this.

Notice small changes and comment positively on these.

Develop new, more positive labels for children.

Provide opportunities for the child to experience success – for some this will need to be tangibly acknowledged, e.g. certificates, charts, letters, stars, etc.

Acknowledge feelings – show empathy.

Provide security in consistency and in fairness – have the same behavioural expectations for everyone.

Celebrate diversity in active ways – everyone is unique and special.

Avoid making value judgements based on family, culture, ethnicity or gender.

The things we say to children

What we say and how we say it to children establishes and defines the quality of the relationship we have with them.

Tell children what you want them to do rather than focusing on what they actually may be doing. A focus on the negative reinforces unwanted behaviour and can promote unhelpful labelling. Acknowledging feelings validates the child but does not excuse poor behaviour. Giving the child some choice promotes responsibility in making decisions. Give positive feedback wherever possible. 'Catch the child being good' and give him a sense of hope that he can be successful.

Helpful phrases

'You seem to be having some difficulty here./What should you be doing? Tell me.'

'What would help?/How can I help?'

'What you did manage to do was fine.' Or 'I like the way you . . .'

'I can see that you are feeling upset. (But the rule is . . .)'

'No-one is allowed to hurt other children here, you are not allowed to hurt anyone and no-one is allowed to hurt you.'

'What might you do to make it better? What do *you* think should happen next?'

'I'll give you a few moments to think about this/settle down/calm down.'

'Tomorrow is another day – we'll try again then.'

Unhelpful phrases

'Why can't you . . . always be like this?/be like . . ./do as you are told for once?'

'Why do you never/always . . .?/What's the matter with you?'

'You're just over-reacting.'

'Of course it's not difficult.'

'How many times do I have to tell you?/I'm sick and tired . . ./You're not the only one in this class.'

Involving parents/carers

The first approach to families about a child whose behaviour is giving cause for concern will have a major impact on the establishment of a good working relationship between home and school. The best chance of successful intervention is when parents and teachers can work together. Parents who are used to coming to school to hear positive things said about their children and generally feel welcomed and valued are likely to be more willing to discuss difficulties when they do arise.

It is helpful to think through the aims for a first meeting. This could be some or all of the following:

- to share mutual concerns;
- to throw light on the difficulties the child is experiencing;
- to explore and confirm strengths and competencies for the child and the family;
- to share ideas for improving matters;
- to find out if referrals have been made elsewhere;
- to suggest sources of help, perhaps, and support for the family if this is appropriate and wanted.

Families who fear that the purpose of the discussion is to attribute blame or say how terrible their child is may understandably become defensive and/or avoid coming into school. Although it is an important perspective for the teacher it is also not helpful to talk about the needs of the other children in the class. Focus on the needs of the child in question.

An informal verbal approach from the class teacher is usually better than a formal letter and raises less anxiety. Ask parents if you can have a chat about how their child is getting along and ask them to suggest a convenient time. If a parent/carer has difficulties with the English language she may like to bring someone with her to help interpret or for support. Others may also appreciate the opportunity to bring a friend along.

Before the meeting, have chairs arranged so that the teacher will not be behind a desk and try to ensure that there will be no interruptions. It may be useful to plan for someone to take care of younger children or at least have something for them to play with.

The discussion

First state your expectation for the length of the meeting and ask how much time parents/carers have available for the meeting. Decide on a time to finish and stick to it.

Say why you have asked to meet with the parents/carers; it may be useful to frame this in terms of needing their help so that you can understand their child better and do what is best for him at school. Parents will become defensive if you start by persuading them how difficult their child is. They will then be unable to hear what you have to say.

Say something positive about the child.

Then say why you are concerned by focusing on the child's needs; don't list their wrongdoings, e.g. say 'I wondered if there might be something bothering Patrick? He seems to be having some difficulties keeping his temper at the moment.'

Ask the parent/carer for her views, e.g. 'Do you have any concerns about him at home?'

You may want to ask whether the parent/carer knows of anything which might help the child. (If she suggests something which you feel is inappropriate say that this is not something which would work in school.)

Enquire about any changed circumstances at home, e.g. 'Do you know of anything which might be upsetting him?' This may be a sensitive question and parents/carers may not want to tell you about difficulties at a first meeting. If a positive relationship is established, however, they may feel more comfortable in doing so another time. Let the parents/carers know that unless it is a child protection issue you will not break their confidences. It is important to be vigilant about this or you may lose both their trust and possibly that of other parents/carers.

If relevant ask about eating/sleeping, e.g. 'He seems very tired, especially in the morning – do you think he's getting enough sleep?'

If relevant find out if there are any medical concerns, e.g. 'Has he had his hearing checked lately?'

If relevant ask about the child's history, e.g. 'How many years has he been at school in this country?'

Actions

Agree some action by the end of the meeting. It is important to emphasise that the child needs understanding and help, not punishment. Actions do not have to be anything detailed or difficult. At this stage the simpler the better, e.g.

- give her lots of praise for sharing;
- keep an eye on her for a while;
- talk to her about . . .
- ask her how she feels about . . .
- try to get her to bed a bit earlier;

- get some better information about what might be going on, e.g. observe in the playground for a week or two.

Some actions will be for the teacher, some for parents and some will be carried out both at school and at home.

Simply raising the family's awareness may be helpful. If the parents offer to do anything at home it must be something that they can really manage. Parents who have other family or work commitments may agree things that are not realistic. They may then feel guilty and not come to further meetings. Check: 'Will you be able to manage that?'

Keep brief notes of the meeting, especially the agreed actions. It may be better to do this in the last few minutes with the parents as a review of what has been said. If you are noting anything of a more personal nature check with the parents first that this is acceptable. It is a courtesy to let families know what will happen to anything written down at a meeting.

Follow up

Always arrange a follow up meeting before the parents leave. Remind them a few days before this next meeting either verbally or with a short note.

If the child is now behaving well then the meeting provides an opportunity for positive feedback. If difficulties continue then this provides an opportunity to think about the next step – which will usually be school action/individual education plan.

Evaluation of plans

Although there are a number of possible plans to consider here, the most effective will be those which are linked closely to assessment. Regular reviews of intervention are an important part of ongoing assessment. They provide good information about what is working, what needs to change and what could be developed further. Behaviour may improve straight away or may worsen temporarily so it is wise to maintain a consistent programme for at least six weeks before evaluating it. Involving both the child and the parents in a review meeting gives an opportunity to celebrate even small successes. It may be useful to incorporate a rating scale to discuss where the situation was at the beginning of the plan, where it is now and what might be put in place to move towards an even more positive outcome. Acknowledging all positive developments and recognising good feelings about progress is a great motivation to keep going.

Part Two: Settling to Work

This part deals with children who may have difficulty getting themselves organised, listening to and following teacher directions, settling to work, staying on-task and completing activities. These children often take up a great deal of teacher time and may also disrupt the work of others. The frequency, persistency and duration of even low-level disruption can at times be a major source of teacher stress. Additionally, such behaviours eventually have a major impact on the achievement not only of the student engaged in the behaviour, but also of their classmates.

Many children who have difficulties with settling to work may be uncertain of what to do or they may be unable to complete the work set. They may not be used to associating work with good feelings and a sense of satisfaction from the completion of tasks and hence are reluctant to start. Some children when they first attend school may be distracted by the wealth of equipment/materials in the busy classroom and flit from activity to activity. Others may be at a developmental stage where they are much more self-directed. Children who are very anxious will also have trouble directing and maintaining their focus on given tasks. A few children may have an underlying condition that is contributing to their inability to settle. It is best to avoid jumping to this conclusion. Alternative explanations need to be explored in the first instance and interventions established and evaluated.

General good practice lies in:

- checking whether the expectation of the child is at the right level – not all children in the same age cohort will be at the same developmental level;
- making it very clear to the child what he is expected to do and helping him to begin the task;
- building on what the child can already do;
- ensuring that work is set in small, manageable steps;
- using multi-sensory methods where possible to match teaching to individual learning styles;
- providing visual support, modelling, asking other, more competent children to help;
- clarifying that the child knows what constitutes 'finished';
- giving opportunities to practise and generalise skills;

- giving positive feedback for success;
- focusing on effort rather than on the end product.

Some children are resistant to direction from the teacher, particularly if they are used to not responding to adults or are frequently left to their own devices in other settings. These children may need to have limited choices, e.g. the order in which things are done, so that they can have some measure of control.

For some children, it is beneficial to ensure and raise awareness of feelings of satisfaction, achievement and pride in their work. This means that they require regular opportunities to succeed. These may need to be structured by the teacher, with regular positive feedback about progress. Developing a classroom ethos in which promoting self-efficacy and raising self-esteem are high priorities is therefore essential.

* Starred suggestions in the following tables are explained on pages 11 to 18.

DIFFICULTIES LISTENING TO AND FOLLOWING INSTRUCTIONS

Behaviour	Assessment	Short-Term Management Strategies	Intervention Plans for Longer-Term Change
Problem Behaviour Student demonstrates difficulty listening to/following instructions. **Target Behaviour** To pay attention to teacher and focus on task given.	*Context Check: hearing, receptive language skills (in first language as well as English if relevant). Does the child have dual attention channels? Does she need to focus on one at a time, either on listening *or* on doing? Does the student listen initially/not at all? Is the session/introduction to the task too long? Which activities does the child settle to easily? Are there reasons for this? What is the child like at home?	Locate the pupil so she is near an adult. Give and maintain good eye contact. Use verbal and visual prompts. *Proximity praise Use the child's name within a general sentence to the whole group. Give short, clear instructions. Give one instruction at a time if necessary. Give *Visual cues to support oral instructions. Use repetition, paraphrasing. Start the child with something that is already familiar and manageable then 1:1 instructions when others in the class are settled. Give one task at a time. Ask the pupil to repeat the instruction and ask what she is going to do first. Give praise for any steps in the right direction. Is there another student who can help explain or do the activity with the child?	Ensure good match between student's ability and expectations of task. Ensure child experiences success – however limited. Establish and practise listening skills. Use reminders for 'good' listening – where do we look, where do we put our hands, etc? Reinforce skills regularly. Use listening games that help cue into auditory information and raise motivation. Build on motivation and interest. Set up workstations with minimum distractions/locate the pupil in area of room with least distractibility. Give consideration to classroom layout. For older students, set up self-monitoring. Use visual cue cards linked to instructions: * Symbol system. Set up more formal peer support. * 'Paula Pane' – teacher talks to 'imaginary pupil' drawn on the window. Shorter 'carpet times'/introduction /plenary sessions may be necessary.

31

AVOIDANCE STRATEGIES

Behaviour	Assessment	Short-Term Management Strategies	Intervention Plans for Longer-Term Change
Problem Behaviour Student engages in avoidance strategies e.g. re-sharpening pencils, going to the toilet. ***Target Behaviour*** To focus on directed task. **In order to do this the child may need to learn to feel confident about beginning work activities.**	*Context Are specific activities avoided? In which situations does the child work best? Are instructions and task clearly understood and accessible by the child? Ascertain how child feels about the activity. Are all necessary resources available to children at appropriate times? Does the child have specific needs with regard to toiletting?	Refocus the student on the task given. Ask what he will be doing next. Start the task with him if necessary. Praise the child for the extent to which he has complied with directions. Use the child as an example to the class whenever he has settled to work. Ensure that all equipment is on the table/desk, so that there is no reason for pupil to leave his place. *Use Conditional directions: 'When you've finished your work, *then* you can sharpen the pencils.' Clarify class rules such as toilet times. Ask the child to tell you the rule and prompt him if necessary.	Start the student on a practical or practice task prior to one that may be more demanding and provide positive feedback for following directions. Give pupil a relevant responsibility, e.g. keeping the pencils sharp – for a particular time in the day. Give paired/small group tasks with a clear role for the child. *Traffic lights *Personal best Establish clear routines for different ways of working. Teach children the details of what they should do and how they should do it. Ensure all students are familiar with expectations about movement around the class, or leaving the classroom. Give positive recognition to those pupils who settle down quickly to directed activities. Teach/encourage students to ask for help when the task is unclear.

POOR ORGANISATION

Behaviour	Assessment	Short-Term Management Strategies	Intervention Plans for Longer-Term Change
Problem Behaviour Very disorganised, the student rarely has the right equipment to begin tasks. ***Target Behaviour*** To have the necessary equipment for the task. **In order to do this, the student will need to know what equipment / materials are required for each task, know where things are kept and remember to bring what they need with her.** **In general the student needs to become increasingly independent.**	*Context Does the student forget many things? What is remembered? Does the child have memory problems for basic skills? Is there a sequencing difficulty? Does the child know where things are kept? Does the pupil know what the task entails? *Organisational competencies	*Proximity praise to remind child. Check equipment at beginning of activity. Ask child what she needs for the activity. Focus on organisation for one activity at a time. A checklist stuck to the desk/table as a reminder may help to make decisions about what equipment is necessary. Use verbal prompts and praise. Use visual prompts/reminders for specific activities.	Teach routines for where things are kept – where to put things after an activity, so that they can be found readily next time. Give a responsibility for tidying away/giving out equipment. *Mnemonics and memory games Use a colour code/symbol for all the equipment needed for a particular activity. Work closely with home on reminders for things to be brought to school, e.g. a 'prompt' list on the front door which lists what is needed for each day. The child should be involved in making this. Work with family on the development of child's independence, e.g. instead of doing things for the child, an adult starts, and the child then continues. Teach pupils about planning – for a range of purposes.

33

HELPLESSNESS

Behaviour	Assessment	Short-Term Management Strategies	Intervention Plans for Longer-Term Change
Problem Behaviour Student says, 'I can't', perhaps before an attempt has been made. Helplessness Getting others to do the task or copying. **Target Behaviour** The child makes at least initial attempts to work independently. **To do this the child will need to feel increasingly successful and effective.**	*Context What are the circumstances when the student does not behave in this way? Are there clear reasons for this? Is he more successful when working: individually, in a small group, or whole class? Ask parents for information about what the child does for himself at home. Is the child used to having things done for him at home? Check that work and teacher expectations match the pupil's ability.	Present task in smaller segments. Explain task in terms of what is already familiar, and reiterate similarities. Reflect on when the child was successful in a similar activity. Use the expression 'We can', start the work with the student and explain that you will return in . . . minutes. Differentiated work and expectations – ensure pupil knows purpose of work. • content • presentation • accuracy Ensure it is within his capabilities. Frequent praise for each small step achieved. Self-evaluation of achievements. Focus initially on effort rather than outcome.	Value work of all levels, by displaying on the walls/notice board. Develop an 'I can' book for the child, with work samples/photographs and refer to it, to provide a reminder of the child's achievements. Build confidence – highlighting the student's achievements to others *Personal best Involve pupils in record keeping, work samples. Use visual records showing progress and development over time to remind child of improvements. Use alternative methods of recording work, e.g. computer, scribe, tape recorder and graphics. Increase the use of shared/paired activities, with differing roles. Structure opportunities for the pupil to help younger children occasionally. Promote the acceptance of mistakes as part of the learning process, e.g. drafting and re-drafting. Admit that even adults can get things wrong/make mistakes. Work closely with parents to ensure that appropriate expectations are made and positive feedback for effort given.

REFUSAL TO COOPERATE

Behaviour	Assessment	Short-Term Management Strategies	Intervention Plans for Longer-Term Change
Problem Behaviour Refusal to cooperate with instructions. ***Target Behaviour*** Positive responses to teacher directions. **In order to do this the student will need to learn to be motivated about cooperating.**	*Context Is task matched with ability? Is refusal a way of maintaining self-esteem? *Perceptions *ABC *Tally Where/with whom is child most cooperative and least cooperative? Is this a sudden change in behaviour? Has there been a recent upset at home/change at school? *Competencies	Calmly restate expectations. Clarify purpose of tasks in a way which child can relate to. Give the student a limited choice. Move away and give time to comply. *Proximity praise to two children who are cooperating. Clarify *Consequences of behaviour as choice. *Tactical ignoring. Avoid public confrontations – follow up without an audience. *Take Two – suggest a phrase the child uses such as 'I can have a go at that'. If this behaviour is unusual, talk with the child after the class to find out what is bothering her. If the child is unwilling to explain, leave channels of communication open. The child may talk at a later date.	Explain and discuss rules for cooperation with the whole class. Play 'cooperative games' with the whole class and small groups including the child concerned. *Circle work to focus on cooperation and the group. Reinforce helpful cooperative behaviour by commentary and specific praise. Promote a positive self-image by giving the pupil opportunities to enjoy and be successful at cooperation at both academic and non-academic tasks. Use stars, merits, incentives and reward systems. *Marbles in the jar Relate tasks to the child's interests where possible, e.g. TV programmes, pets, computer games.

35

FLITTING FROM ONE ACTIVITY TO ANOTHER

Behaviour	Assessment	Short-Term Management Strategies	Intervention Plans for Longer-Term Change
Problem Behaviour Flitting from one activity to another. **Target Behaviour** To focus on one thing at a time.	*Context Does this happen with all tasks? Which activities engage the pupil most? How long does the child stay with a favoured activity? *Tally Check overall level of ability – is it just writing tasks that the student avoids? What does the child concentrate on at home/for how long? Are things happening at home/in the playground which may be affecting concentration? Is the classroom too noisy/distracting?	Consider locating the student so that adults can intervene quickly. Check the child has everything he needs. Re-state expectations. Use *Conditional language – 'when . . . then . . .' Give positive attention when the pupil stays with an activity. Organise one or two short-term teacher directed tasks of specific duration, followed by free choice. Build on what the student is already doing; then self-directed activity (time-limited) then the teacher directed activity. Give the student limited choices.	Consider classroom management to limit distractibility, e.g. setting up workstations for individual students in quiet areas. Clarify classroom rules for moving around, e.g. to take messages, give out books, etc. Ensure that the child understands the concept of 'finished' in relation to specific tasks (which must be within the child's capabilities). Encourage use of a 'finished' basket, into which pupil puts completed work before moving onto another activity. Give different activities with the same learning goal. Encourage self-monitoring, e.g. large egg timers, checklists/symbols so that the child understands the order of tasks. Use positive reinforcement for whole class for completion of activities, e.g. *Marbles in the jar. Establish peer support to maintain a focus on the task in hand. Encourage parents to reinforce the idea that everyday activities must be completed or maintained for a specific and manageable period.

DISTRACTED BY OTHERS

Behaviour	Assessment	Short-Term Management Strategies	Intervention Plans for Longer-Term Change
Problem Behaviour The child is constantly distracted by other students. **Target Behaviour** To focus on task in hand.	*Context Which pupils? What are relationships like with other pupils? Does the child aspire to be a friend of these pupils? When are distractions most/ least likely to occur?	Re-affirm classroom rules. Minimise distractions/noises where possible. Relocate the student away from a particular group. If appropriate, ask the child where she would like to sit in order to work better/with whom she would like to sit. Praise the student for times when she is focused. Verbally re-focus child's attention, using her name when giving general class directions.	Re-think classroom organisation and timetabling constraints. Locate student away from others/activities that are distracting. An individual workstation *may* be useful if the pupil is generally easily distracted. Beware of further isolating the child. Place the student near to good role models. Teach negotiation skills and provide *Scripts, e.g. 'I'm working now – talk to me later'. Give opportunities as appropriate for students to work/play in different groupings, with children they would not normally pair up with. Promote class ethos/routines for 'working quietly'. The teacher can use visual illustrations for acceptable noise levels, e.g. a 'noise thermometer' with a moving pointer or *Traffic lights. *Problem-solving discussion

NOT FINISHING WORK STARTED

Behaviour	Assessment	Short-Term Management Strategies	Intervention Plans for Longer-Term Change
Problem Behaviour Not finishing work started. ***Target Behaviour*** Child finishes set work. **In order to do this the child needs to learn to understand and share teacher's concept of 'finished' and to feel good about completing activities.** (See also, Flitting from one activity to another.)	*Onset *Context Observation to clarify nature of unfinished tasks. Is the work at an appropriate level ? *ABC Check short-term memory.	Ensure that the student understands what the teacher means by 'finished'. If necessary, be very specific, e.g. 4 lines of handwriting, 10 sentences with a verb, etc. Make clear the primary purpose of the activity: • accuracy • presentation • content. Give praise for effort and progress towards the stated aim. Use a small steps approach – give one part at a time. Some pupils may be overwhelmed by the whole.	*Behaviour charts *Use self-monitoring and negotiation with the student, e.g. number of pieces of work to be completed in one day with a tick sheet and rewards for achievement. * Personal best Set up 'finished' and 'unfinished' workboxes with clear criteria for each. Establish and rehearse routines for work completion, e.g. planning/ redrafting/final work. Model following routines and good organisation. Establish peer support for checking work completion. Link achievement with feelings of pleasure, e.g. showing 'finished' work to teachers/Head teacher/parents/carers. Give consideration to learning-teaching styles, grouping and differentiation.

QUIETLY NOT ENGAGING

Behaviour	Assessment	Short-Term Management Strategies	Intervention Plans for Longer-Term Change
Problem Behaviour Quietly not engaging. Looking blank/keeping head down with little work completion. (This behaviour makes fewer demands on teachers than many others so it is easily overlooked. It does, however, require specific teacher attention.) **Target Behaviour** Child engages with task appropriately or asks for help. (See also other chapters on emotional distress and unusual behaviours.)	Check: Receptive language skills (in first language and English if relevant), hearing, health, amount of sleep. Are there any social and emotional concerns? Is the child engaged socially? Is the task matched to the student's ability? Find out from parents/carers which activities do engage the child. *Perceptions	Ensure that the student knows what to do. Demonstrate what is expected. Start the activity with the child. Give short-term targets with one other student. Discuss with both children afterwards what they did. (Use a positive role model.) Give positive feedback in private to shy pupils.	Build confidence by structuring experiences in which the student can be successful. Address any medical/health/emotional/language concerns. Build social confidence by supervising peer support. Give the student responsibility, perhaps a non-written task as part of a group, e.g. giving out paper at the beginning of an activity. Use the pupil's strengths to build status in the class. Encourage child to seek help using *Traffic lights.

Part Three: General Disruptive Behaviour

Children who display general disruptive behaviour do so for one or more reasons:

- they have learnt that negative behaviours gain attention which they find rewarding;
- they have simply not learnt what is expected in a classroom or to take notice of adult requests;
- they are impulsive and have not yet learnt to control voice and/or body movements;
- they are unable, or believe they are unable, to comply with teacher requests and expectations so do other things instead.

All children need attention. For some children, attention for negative behaviour is better than no attention at all. It soon becomes clear to many children that certain behaviours, such as playing quietly, are ignored by adults while others, such as whining, silliness or irritating other children, guarantee them maximum attention. This way of behaving may have become well established by the time these children start school, and it may take consistency, patience and time to help such a child believe that other positive behaviours will bring the adult attention they need.

Whatever may be acceptable elsewhere, children need to know exactly which behaviours are appropriate for school. This may not be clear to them. Teaching behaviours and routines in a structured way and giving attention to those who behave appropriately is therefore essential.

There are children who have experienced inconsistent management by the adults in their lives – neither threats nor promises are carried out consistently, so children learn to pay little attention to what adults say. Teachers need to ensure that they say what they mean and mean what they say – without offering rewards or issuing consequences that later do not materialise. By implication, these should be simple to administer in the busy classroom, and graded, so that whatever the circumstances, there is always an appropriate reward or sanction available.

Many children who are disruptive may be seeking ways of gaining peer attention and approval although their actions may have the opposite effect. These students need to learn skills which enable them to relate more appropriately to others in the class. It is important that all children feel that they are valued members of the class group.

On the other hand, the 'outrageous' behaviour of pupils who take the role of 'class-clown' – daring to do things that others would not – may be compensating for their inability to feel good about their performance in terms of the formal curriculum. These students need to gain status through more acceptable ways of behaving, and to feel better about themselves as individuals. Concerns about the behaviour of some students may distract attention from the fact that they have learning or other difficulties – this must always be given consideration as part of any formulation about the behaviour of students. It is always useful to check whether the child is really able to meet the expectations in the classroom and then, if necessary, structure situations in which the child can have a greater chance to be successful.

Although the behaviour of a particular student may not make sense to the teacher it will *in most cases* make sense to the child in terms of some pay-off. It is always worth asking the question, 'What is this pupil getting out of behaving in this way?'

Some children have trouble keeping their hands, feet and voices under control. These children need to raise awareness of what they are doing with a focus on developing efficacy. Using narrative techniques that talk about the problem as something separate from the child may help. 'Who's in charge here – you or your feet? You tell them what they can and can't do!' This is discussed further as 'externalising problems' in the Introduction.

Where there is regular communication between school and home about when things are going well, then parents/carers are far more likely to be supportive when difficulties arise. Regular communication enables difficulties to be 'nipped in the bud', providing an opportunity to share strategies with parents/carers, to discuss with them the importance of maintaining consistency, so that there is increased chance of success with any interventions that are put in place. Where parents are able to be involved in a reward system for improved behaviour it may be useful to think in terms of 'attention' rewards, such as time together doing something specific. Before this is put in place it is crucial that everyone feels confident that promises can and will be fulfilled.

* Starred suggestions in the following tables are explained in the Introduction.

PUSHING/POKING OTHER CHILDREN

Behaviour	Assessment	Short-Term Management Strategies	Intervention Plans for Longer-Term Change
Problem Behaviour Pushing/poking other children. **Target Behaviour** To keep hands and feet to themselves. **In order to do this the child may need to learn to be aware of personal space, to establish contact with other children appropriately and to improve attention and listening skills.**	*Duration *ABC In which circumstances does the child *not* poke or push other children? What is different then? Does the student know how to establish social interactions? *Context: Which children? *Frequency Is the pupil aware of this behaviour? Is the student being asked to sit still for too long? Is the child being bullied?	*Proximity praise Give *"The Look' Move near student and/or locate the student where there is least opportunity to poke/push others. * 'Shape' wanted behaviour Give a reminder/warning then: Offer *Consequences as a choice, e.g. removal from group: 'If you continue to do that you are choosing to sit somewhere else.' Say, 'Your hands/feet seem to be out of control – please tell them what to do, it's up to you, not to them.'	Clarify rules and routines and give students opportunities to practise, e.g. 'On the carpet we sit with our hands in our lap or our arms folded like this.' Set up sessions for pairs/individuals, with an adult, to learn and practise *when* to initiate interaction with other children and *how* to do this appropriately. Negotiate positive attention/rewards for appropriate behaviour using *Behaviour charts. Ensure a high level of success. Use a pre-agreed, non-verbal signal/reminder when the unwanted behaviour begins, and reinforce good responses to this signal. Depending on the cause, it may be possible to negotiate with pupils so they choose to move to a place where they can sit appropriately. Raise body awareness in PE lessons and individually. *Externalise problems to develop efficacy in body control. For playground problems, teach other students to be assertive and to request that this behaviour stops. Ensure that adults in the playground are vigilant. Address bullying issues.

FIDGETY BEHAVIOUR

Behaviour	Assessment	Short-Term Management Strategies	Intervention Plans for Longer-Term Change
Problem Behaviour General fidgety behaviour while others are speaking and which disrupts others. **Target Behaviour** To focus on the teacher and listen appropriately.	* Context In which situations is this worse? When does it not happen? Is the child hungry? Is diet an issue? *Frequency *Duration Check child's understanding and possible anxiety levels. Is the behaviour a habit? Is the child aware of the behaviour? Is the child expected to sit for too long?	Re-state expectations in class for good sitting and listening. *Proximity praise Re-focus by using the child's name within a general sentence, e.g. 'We are all going to practise, Carl, our spellings from yesterday.' Acknowledge immediately when the child shows you he is focused. Give visual support/stimulus to auditory input where possible.	Let the student know that you are concerned about his fidgety behaviour and why it is a problem. If appropriate, *Mirror the behaviour. Ask what will help him to keep still or how he can stop bothering others. Agree non-verbal reminders with the child, e.g. when he is fidgeting you will hold up one finger to remind him to settle down. Teach listening skills and give practice at listening activities, e.g. tell stories in which children have to do an action whenever a certain name or item is mentioned. Provide 'worry beads' or similar displacement activities, for those pupils who need tactile stimulation. Build in kinaesthetic activities and opportunity for physical movement, as part of the timetable. Give consideration to where the pupil sits. Relocate the child, or let him choose somewhere that will be less distracting to others. Reduce the length of activities.

MAKING NOISES

Behaviour	Assessment	Short-Term Management Strategies	Intervention Plans for Longer-Term Change
Problem behaviour Making noises **Target behaviour** Keeping quiet and participating verbally as appropriate. **In order to do this the child may need to learn appropriate social behaviour and raise awareness of her own actions.**	*Context *ABC How aware is the child of this behaviour? Is it deliberate? Can the student give a reason for the behaviour? Check language development/hearing. Is this part of a cluster of behaviours?	Say the child's name and give *'The Look' or an agreed signal. Reinforce appropriate behaviour by stating what you want the student to do. If the child continues to make noises ask her to stop. Give *Take-up time – a chance to comply. Give a warning. Offer *Consequences as a choice. *Tactically ignore If this happens during a whole-class session, say that everyone needs to be quiet before you will continue with the lesson. You may wish to pass this message around the group rather than speak above the noise. Give recognition to all children as they get the message and sit quietly. Encourage the student to have a 'good shout' in the playground – making a noise in an appropriate place at an appropriate time.	Use *Mirroring and teach appropriate behaviour. Teach peers not to reinforce the behaviour by copying/laughing. Agree non-verbal prompts to remind the child of expected behaviour. Give child opportunities to be listened to, to participate appropriately. Show to the child and to the class that you value the child's positive contributions. If the child has gained esteem by being the class-clown then other ways to maintain the child's self-esteem need to be put in place. Give opportunities to develop and display related strengths, e.g. an appropriate use of humour. Class discussion about behaviour in different situations, what is appropriate at one time and place is not in another. Use *Traffic lights, to monitor noise level generally, perhaps in conjunction with *Marbles in the jar.

ATTENTION-SEEKING SILLINESS

Behaviour	Assessment	Short-Term Management Strategies	Intervention Plans for Longer-Term Change
Problem Behaviour General attention-seeking silliness. **Target Behaviour** Student will seek to gain attention by behaving appropriately. **In order to do this the student needs to learn which positive behaviours will consistently bring attention rewards in school.**	*Context *ABC Is attention sought from peers/adults/both? What is behaviour like at home and how do parents/carers respond? Is this work avoidance? Is there any evidence of an underlying reason why the child needs a high level of attention? *Competencies	*Tactically ignore unwanted behaviour. *Proximity praise *'The Look'. Re-state class rules/expectations. Give *Take-up time. Give warning/reminder, then give *Consequences as a choice. *Time-out	For some children, exaggerated 'larger than life' responses to wanted behaviour are helpful but only if the adult is comfortable with this, e.g. 'Hey wow – look how well Michael is sitting this morning.' Care is needed not to reinforce the unwanted behaviour or appear insincere. Give opportunities to develop strengths and also to take a lead in some activities. Give specific praise for responsible behaviour. Encourage the child to monitor his own behaviour, with regular reviews with the teacher. Structure opportunities for success, so that the child gains esteem and status for more appropriate behaviours. Structure peer support and place the pupil alongside positive role models. Teach other children to ignore silliness. Clarify what this means. Invest in good home–school liaison to ensure that this behaviour is not reinforced at home. Encourage a focus on the desired behaviour.

FREQUENT INTERRUPTIONS

Behaviour	Assessment	Short-Term Management Strategies	Intervention Plans for Longer-Term Change
Problem Behaviour Frequent interruptions **Target Behaviour** To wait her turn and participate appropriately within the group. **In order to do this the child may need to learn to raise social awareness, develop social skills and seek attention appropriately.**	*Context When is this behaviour at its worst? In what circumstances does the child not interrupt? *ABC *Frequency *Tally What is child like at home and what do parents/carers do when interrupted?	State expectations at the start of each lesson with regard to when it is appropriate to contribute verbally or ask questions. Re-state expectations when interrupted/ask child to tell you. *Proximity praise for those who await turn/do not interrupt: 'I see that Jem has been waiting to ask a question – what do you want to say, Jem?' Give minimal attention to the child who is interrupting but turn to her quickly when she waits appropriately, e.g. puts her hand up. One way of giving minimal attention is for the teacher to make a badge or a label which says 'not now' (this could include the child's name). When the child interrupts she can tap the badge without looking at the child. Responding promptly and positively to the child when she has waited quietly will reinforce the appropriate behaviour.	Discuss, establish and give opportunities to practise classroom rules and routines. Clarify in detail how the child can gain teacher attention – give opportunities to rehearse and practise the behaviour. Use visual aids for children to indicate when they need help with work. If appropriate, ask pupils to seek help from a peer, rather than ask an adult, initially. Make sure the child knows that she will get her turn if she behaves appropriately and then ensure that this does happen. Teach listening skills. Use *Circle work to raise awareness of taking turns. Highlight the child's developing skills in appropriate listening by using her as a model for others. *Behaviour chart Share the strategy with parents/carers to maintain consistency.

OVER-THE-TOP BEHAVIOURS

Behaviour	Assessment	Short-Term Management Strategies	Intervention Plans for Longer-Term Change
Problem Behaviour Over-the-top behaviour – this is where the child's behaviour is not inappropriate in itself but is louder, longer, or more excessive than is appropriate in the classroom and disrupts others.	* ABC * Frequency *Onset *Perception – why does this make sense to the child? *Monitor triggers and patterns.	Stand close to the child and use a physical prompt when behaviour begins. If the pupil is likely to be responsive, a gentle touch on the hand, arm or shoulders may be calming. Be aware, however, that for some children, physical contact may be unwelcome and exacerbate problems. Speak quietly and raise awareness of the inappropriateness of his behaviour.	Discuss and reinforce differences between behaviour in a range of contexts. What is OK on the sports field is not OK in school. Work with the child in setting targets. Use rating scales so that he can begin to tune into his own behaviour and self-monitor. Agree a non-verbal reminder with the child.
Target Behaviour Appropriate classroom behaviour. **In order to do this, the child may need to learn to modify his responses and behaviours and understand what is appropriate for school contexts. He may also need to find other ways of gaining attention.** **(See also Emotional distress.)**	Who else is involved? *Ability Could this be a work avoidance strategy? Check hearing	Give reminders of rules of behaviour, e.g. for play fights which can easily turn into real fights. Calmly state expectations of behaviour and consequences. *Take Two Avoid giving attention for negative behaviour, use *Time-out. If necessary, remove from audience – perhaps to another classroom.	Develop peer support – mentor system or *Circle of friends. Use relaxation techniques with the class, to enable them to compare states of agitation and calmness. Teach the pupil concerned to recognise bodily signs of agitation/excitement, etc. and then to modify the behaviour. Ensure that work is at an appropriate level. Ensure the child gets opportunities to gain the attention of the class appropriately, perhaps by having a role of responsibility. If this is a work avoidance strategy, ensure that at least some of the work is completed in the child's time.

OUTRIGHT DEFIANCE

Behaviour	Assessment	Short-Term Management Strategies	Intervention Plans for Longer-Term Change
Problem Behaviour Outright defiance ***Target Behaviour*** Cooperation with teacher directions. **In order to do this the child may need to learn alternative ways to be in control of aspects of her life, that she does not have to always 'win out' with adults. She will need to learn to follow direction and how to negotiate.**	*Onset *ABC *Frequency Can the child do what is being asked? Will the child 'lose face' by complying? *Perception Why does this make sense to the child?	Stay calm – resist taking the child's behaviour personally. Moderate pitch and tone of voice so that it stays low, i.e. stay calm yourself. Maintain an appropriate distance from the child – too close may be perceived as threatening. Turn your body sideways to minimise perceived threat. Don't get into a 'win or lose' situation. *Conflict management Use *Partial agreement and *Take-up time. Use 'I' statements, not 'you' statements, e.g. 'I want you to . . .' not 'You should be . . .' Acknowledge that you can't 'make' the child do something. Give choices. Where appropriate give *Consequences as a choice. Divert any audience where possible. Focus on the rest of the class as much as possible, but do not compromise safety.	Use a one-to-one setting when adult and student are calm, to ask, 'Tell me what the problem is/what was going on there? What was making you feel uncomfortable about doing as you were asked?' Use a positive comment about the child to start the conversation, and use the session to show concern – not to reprimand. Ensure tasks match ability and the student is not refusing because of fears of failure. Model that making mistakes is part of learning. Give prior notice of more challenging tasks; link these to what pupil can already do. Focus on effort rather than results. An individual reward system *Behaviour chart may be appropriate for some pupils. Teach and model *Conflict management and negotiation skills. Build on the relationship with the child over time. Show interest, be available to listen, don't judge, build trust.

RUDENESS

Behaviour	Assessment	Short-Term Management Strategies	Intervention Plans for Longer-Term Change
Problem Behaviour Rudeness **Target Behaviour** Student speaks to adults appropriately.	*Onset * ABC *Frequency *Perception Level of rudeness, how overt/covert? Is this impacting negatively on the class?	*Tactical ignoring. Ask the child if he intended to be rude. Some children do not perceive their behaviour to be intentionally disrespectful. Clarify the messages he is giving by his words and expressions. State that the rudeness is unacceptable and ask what could have been said instead. *'Take Two': 'Cut. Perhaps a better way would be to say . . . Now would you like to have a go – take two?' State that you speak to students with respect and expect the same from them. If the student does admit that the behaviour was intentional then ask what he hoped would be the outcome. It is possible that the child is angry with others and finds the adults in school an easier target. If this is the case then look at management and intervention in 'Emotional Distress'.	Discuss what 'respect' means with the class and how people need to treat each other. Discuss differences in interactions, e.g. how you might talk to a mate would be different from how you might speak to an adult in school. *Circle time activities to reinforce appropriate interactions. *Problem-solving discussion. Model respectful interactions with pupils even when they are behaving in unacceptable ways.

Part Four: Social Interactions

There are some children in school whose difficult behaviour appears to be centred on their poor relationships with others, especially their peers. They always seem to be getting into arguments and conflicts and are frequently 'in trouble' in the playground and other less structured times of the day.

Such behaviour needs very careful assessment, especially observation in different contexts. It may be that the behaviour is reactive and there is an element of provocation or rejection by others. Interventions should be interactive and involve the way all children *think* about friendly behaviour as well as *teaching* the skills needed to establish or maintain positive relationships.

A sense of 'belonging' is now recognised to be a strong factor in promoting resilience and psychological well-being – and hence positive behaviours. Promoting inclusion in the class is therefore a central tenet of addressing social difficulties.

Children need to be aware of the messages they give to others. What they say, how they behave, facial expressions and 'body language' all give messages. These are on the continuum from friendly invitations to social contact to indications of hostility.

A major tool for learning is copying. Where children have had poor models of social interaction then they urgently need alternative models where other, more positive ways of interacting are demonstrated. This will begin with the adults in school – how they behave towards each other and how they speak, listen and relate to the children.

The school and class ethos makes a great deal of difference in how children can get to know each other, how they are included in activities, how differences are valued and how self-esteem is maintained. There are many equal opportunities issues to be taken into consideration. How well people 'get on' with each other is not only important for cooperative activity and promoting learning, it is also at the crux of much personal happiness or misery, both in childhood and later on. It requires a high priority in schools and positive social behaviour may need to be taught in structured ways. A focus on raising self-esteem and self-confidence is integral to this. Peers need encouragement to acknowledge changes in others as negative labelling often reinforces antisocial behaviours.

Children need to know that in any social situation there are choices to be made, and that some choices lead to better outcomes than others. Raising awareness of children's own goals and teaching them a range of possible ways of thinking and acting is empowering and is a useful first step on the road to becoming responsible members of society.

* Starred suggestions in the following tables are explained in the Introduction.

NOT TAKING TURNS OR SHARING

Behaviour	Assessment	Short-Term Management Strategies	Intervention Plans for Longer-Term Change
Problem Behaviour Not demonstrating ability to take turns/share. **Target Behaviour** Initially student takes turns and shares within a pair and then builds on this. **Child needs to understand that being able to share is in her best interests, e.g. other pupils will be more likely to want to play with her.**	*Context At what level can the child take turns/share and in which circumstances? What is the child finding most difficult to share – adult time and attention, class resources or personal items? Where does child show most skills? If this is a changed behaviour, check changes in home circumstances. *Perception	*Proximity praise Ask student if she understands what sharing/taking turns means and ask her to demonstrate. Give positive recognition for being able to share. Negotiations with the child: 'Do you need this – how long do you need it? When can someone else use it?' Re-state class expectations, e.g. 'In this class we all take turns – you have had your turn, I want you to let . . . have a turn now.' *Take Two Clarify consequences of sharing, e.g. other children will want you in their group. Are you expecting too many students to use limited resources? Does there need to be a system which ensures fairness? Give the pupil responsibility for distribution of material/equipment.	Clarify expectations with regard to taking turns and sharing for all children: • What does sharing mean? • Why do we need to learn to share? • Why is sharing sometimes difficult? • What might help us share? Teach skills to individuals initially in a one-to-one setting, allowing for practice in a supervised peer pair. There are many games that foster these skills. Once turn-taking/sharing is established, then extend this to small group work, before generalising to a larger group. Model sharing and give positive recognition to good peer models. Class discussions of lending/ borrowing/taking care of and giving back items. Also sharing time and attention. *Star of the day – a self-esteem raising activity in which everyone gets their turn. Raise awareness of issues by curriculum input, e.g. library lending. Structured (part-supervised) opportunities for learning turn-taking, e.g. role-playing such as planning a party. Use visual support for taking turns, e.g. a chart with a pointer/ alphabetical list.

DOMINANT BEHAVIOUR SUCH AS PUSHING INTO GAMES

Behaviour	Assessment	Short-Term Management Strategies	Intervention Plans for Longer-Term Change
Problem Behaviour Pushing into games, dominant behaviour. **Target Behaviour** Child will participate in groups appropriately.	*Context * ABC *Frequency Careful observation of interactions is necessary here. What is the child actually doing? What are other children doing? *Patterns *Perception *Competencies	Distract the student, where possible, from potential confrontations. *Partial agreement if the child is upset about not being allowed to join – 'I understand what you are saying but . . .' (restate the rule). Raise child's awareness of his own behaviour. Ask: 'What would someone have to do to join your game?' 'What are the rules of this game?' 'What would be a fair way to play?' *Take Two Avoid asking 'Why?', especially when the child may be distressed. Acknowledge that he is upset and when he has calmed down, ask 'What happened here?' Encourage others to be appropriately assertive.	Structure groups so that students mix with a wide range of peers. Make expectations about interactions explicit, e.g. how to join in a game, what pupils should do/say if someone doesn't play properly, how do you decide on rules. Some students may need to be given a specific *Script for certain situations, and opportunity to role-play these before putting them into practice. An ethos in which inclusion is regularly discussed and promoted in all areas of school life. This needs to include class discussion of feelings about being left out. *Problem-solving discussion. Teach friendship skills – raising awareness of what is needed, providing opportunities to practise. Teach structured games in class which students can then use in the playground. Help the child to use dominant tendencies positively – foster leadership skills for other, more appropriate uses.

FIGHTING

Behaviour	Assessment	Short-Term Management Strategies	Intervention Plans for Longer-Term Change
Problem Behaviour Fighting **Target Behaviours** To stop fighting and relate to others positively, using appropriate strategies to manage conflict. To develop impulse control.	*Context *ABC Which students are involved? Is it always the same group? *Tally *Triggers, e.g. something the child is particularly sensitive about and responds to violently Check child's understanding of what is play and what is not, especially where 'rough and tumble' play gets out of hand. If this is a part of a cluster of other difficult behaviours see Emotional distress.	*Time-out Give firm directions to stop to the child who is most likely to comply. Use the child's name – ask another child to tell you if you don't know. Give a second direction saying what you want the child to do, e.g. 'Stand over there'. Send another child for assistance if necessary. Keep calm, shout only for safety reasons. Re-state school rules and consequences. Avoid seeking explanations from children when they are agitated.	Clarify class rules and school rules. Use *Circle work to problem-solve. *Circle of friends Teach *Conflict management skills to the whole class. Teach anger management: • What makes people angry? • Why can anger be a good thing but hurting people is not OK? • What does anger feel like inside? • How do you recognise what makes you angry? • How do you avoid or manage situations which are beginning to make you angry? • What can you do to express anger safely? Teach all children appropriate *Assertiveness strategies, e.g. how to express their needs in non-violent ways.

55

VERBAL BULLYING/NAME CALLING

Behaviour	Assessment	Short-Term Management Strategies	Intervention Plans for Longer-Term Change
Problem Behaviour Verbal bullying/name-calling **Target Behaviour** Child stops calling others hurtful names and relates to them in more positive way. (See also Physical bullying.)	*Context *Frequency Observation: what is actually said, and to whom. Is there provocation/or other contributory factors? Are there underlying racist, sexist views? Monitor frequency and incidence of 'types' of name-calling within the class. Pupils could help with this. Pupil being verbally bullied could record the naming incidents in a logbook. This is useful to clarify the actual incidence of name-calling but may also act as a management strategy.	Acknowledge the insult and focus on feelings. Re-state rules/expectations and ensure that reparations are made later, when the situation has calmed down. Establish this as a *Consequence as choice. When addressing an incident directly, model respectful behaviours to children, especially avoiding any negative labelling. Record the incident briefly and publicly.	Remind and reinforce rules over time. Whole class discussion of: • an agreed definition of verbal bullying; • empathy and feelings about words; • acceptable and unacceptable uses of language; • belonging to groups; • valuing others; • how bystanders can intervene. Give tangible rewards such as badges for children who support others. This maintains awareness. Ask the class what they would like badges to say. Improving the self-esteem of the name-caller may reduce the incidence of name-calling. Teach *Assertiveness skills and strategies for dealing with incidents, e.g. moving towards adults, supportive peers, phrases to say in response. Self-monitoring skills to reassert self-control. Peer *Mediation for conflict resolution. 'Suggestion boxes' for incidents during the week which can then be discussed in *Circle time. Re-affirm equal opportunities policy with parents/carers. The *No-blame approach to bullying

PHYSICAL BULLYING/INTIMIDATION

Behaviour	Assessment	Short-Term Management Strategies	Intervention Plans for Longer-Term Change
Problem Behaviour Physical bullying/intimidation. **Target Behaviour** Child to stop bullying and relate to others positively. (See also Verbal bullying.)	*ABC To whom? Where? Who else is involved? What actually happened? How does the child behave in other contexts? Does the child have positive social relationships? What is the child's perception of this behaviour – what does she expect to gain?	Acknowledge that the child has been bullied and deal with any injury/agitation. Remove children from public arena or remove the audience. Confirm that the behaviour is bullying; do not accept excuses – 'It was only a joke' is only valid if *everyone* is having a good time. Record the incident formally, writing down exactly what happened. Re-state the rule and give appropriate sanction and/or reparations to be made. Some schools use letters of apology by the child to the person they have bullied. These should not be used mechanically or they lose their meaning. With more severe/repeated incidents parents will need to be involved.	Longer-term monitoring/recording. Whole-class discussions to define bullying and identify feelings involved in bullying behaviour: i) at the time ii) afterwards Focus on how this behaviour makes everyone feel uncomfortable, including the bully who might get into trouble, lose friends, not like herself. Raise self-esteem – give child ways of building more positive interactions in the class and taking responsibilities. Talk with the class about responsibilities of all children and how bystander intervention can prevent bullying. Set up and monitor support for the 'survivors of bullying'. Improve monitoring of areas within the school where bullying is most frequent. *No-blame approach

STEALING

Behaviour	Assessment	Short-Term Management Strategies	Intervention Plans for Longer-Term Change
Problem Behaviour Stealing **Target Behaviour** Child does not take things belonging to other people without permission.	*Onset *Frequency What is being taken? From whom? Explore motivation, e.g. hunger, status, attention? Is stealing concealed/revealed? Check level of moral understanding. Does the child realise this is wrong? Does he have a concept of personal property? Have there been changes at home – bereavement or loss? Is this part of a pattern of other concerns about behaviour?	Make it clear that the child is expected to return the items taken. Re-state rules and expectations. It may be useful to ask the child to tell you what these are. Avoid arguments (for denial see appropriate section) and carry out consequences in accordance with school policy. Inform parents as appropriate.	Curriculum input. When does taking, borrowing become stealing? Talk about asking for things and respect for property. Focus on feelings about loss. Amnesties may be helpful for things 'taken by mistake'. Give child opportunities to be 'helpful', attention for positive social behaviours and focus on other ways of raising his status and self-esteem. Reiterate with parents/carers about returning things to school. Deal with any underlying need, e.g. hunger. *Externalising problem.

TRYING TO 'BUY' FRIENDSHIP

Behaviour	Assessment	Short-Term Management Strategies	Intervention Plans for Longer-Term Change
Problem Behaviour Trying to 'buy' friendship (possibly with items not belonging to the child). ***Target Behaviour*** Child needs to learn more appropriate ways of establishing friendships.	*Frequency *ABC Observation over time to identify social relationship issues in the class. Is the child included or rejected in groups? Ascertain the child's level of understanding and overall development. *Perception *Competencies	Talk to the child to clarify her understanding of the situation. Check where the items have come from (see Stealing). Removal of item(s) will depend on value and circumstances but should usually occur. Response will depend on specific incidents, who and what is involved – there may be no need for immediate action.	Be clear about which items are not allowed in school. Talk with children about giving and receiving presents – what is acceptable and what is not. Ensure that children know how to respond to such offers. Checking with/informing the teacher may be appropriate. Check that the parents/carers are not inadvertently colluding. Encourage sharing, and emphasise the need for reciprocity. Discuss perceptions of friendship and teach friendship skills. What makes a good friend? Focus on the value of personal qualities. Focus on improving the self-worth of the child concerned. Highlight alternative friendship strategies – structure peer support.

ALWAYS HAVING TO BE FIRST

Behaviour	Assessment	Short-Term Management Strategies	Intervention Plans for Longer-Term Change
Problem Behaviour Always having to be first. **Target Behaviours** Letting others go first. Waiting appropriately. **In order to do this the child may need to raise his confidence in other ways.**	*Context Is this misplaced enthusiasm? Is the child afraid that he will 'miss out'? Is this part of other social difficulties? Is the child highly competitive in all areas and is this being reinforced?	Remind student of class rules/routines. *Proximity praise Ask child to choose someone to be first. Reverse the line occasionally (the first becomes last). Reassure the child will get his turn. Give positive feedback for enthusiasm but gently re-direct.	Give pupil opportunities to succeed in a role of responsibility and publicly celebrate this success. Acknowledge times when he is not first, or offers a place to another child. Have consistent structures and routines that ensure that everyone has a turn to be first. Raise awareness of the concept of 'fairness' and model this. Offer 'going first' as a reward for other positive behaviours. Play games that have no winners or losers. De-brief on how the players felt about the game. Did it matter that they didn't win? Did they have a good time anyway? Celebrate 'good losers'. Talk about the skills involved in losing and winning well. Provide and raise awareness of those who do this well. Develop a class ethos which values everyone and promotes teamwork.

NEGATIVE ATTITUDE – 'EVERYONE IS AGAINST ME'

Behaviour	Assessment	Short-Term Management Strategies	Intervention Plans for Longer-Term Change
Problem Behaviour 'Everyone's against me.' Negative attitude.	*Onset *Context Who demonstrates positive behaviour towards the child and who is negative?	Acknowledgement of feelings. Ask, 'What makes you think that?' Offer alternative explanations/perceptions.	Set up a log for the student to monitor interactions and focus on positives – this may enable the pupil to recognise her mistaken perceptions. Raise awareness of body language.
Target Behaviours Child develops more positive perceptions and is able to be more positive towards others.	Ascertain views of child's qualities and difficulties from peers.	Re-frame the pupil's ideas, e.g. 'No-one would play with me' to 'You asked Ahmed and Tyrone to play with you, and they were busy.'	Structure group activities in which child can be effective. Give positive feedback.
In order to do this the child needs to feel a valued member of the class group and to develop social confidence.	Are there other concerns about this child? What are these?	Focus on previous positive incidents where possible. Explain that sometimes people don't like what a person does – it doesn't mean that they don't like them. Talk about which behaviours people might like or not like.	Indirect praise, within earshot of the child, but not directly to her is particularly useful if it is to a significant adult. Teach specific skills for establishing friendships. *Star of the day Focus on child's strengths and give opportunities to lead/explain an activity with other children. 'Good news' sessions – opportunities for peer praise for specific acts. Encourage students to give 'Thank you/congratulations' notes to others in the class.

CHEATING

Behaviour	Assessment	Short-Term Management Strategies	Intervention Plans for Longer-Term Change
Problem Behaviour Cheating **Target Behaviour** Child is self-reliant. **In order to do this the child will need to feel successful without cheating.**	*ABC *Frequency Does child understand the 'rules'? Where does the cheating take place – games/work? *Competencies	Don't draw attention to the problem. Give *'The Look' to indicate that you know what is happening. Check everyone's understanding of rules. Check the child knows that what he is doing is cheating – some are genuinely not aware. When the cheating happens during a game, stop the game and ask the group to clarify the rules. Use *Consequences as choice. *Time-out	Class discussions of what cheating is and why it is not a good thing. Where the accepted ethos is highly competitive cheating may seem less important than losing or not achieving high marks. The above may need to be explained to parents to avoid unreasonable pressure. Encourage the class to invent own games with discussion of the rules. If child cheats in work situations he needs to have work at a level at which success can be achieved. Avoid situations which may publicise the child's weaknesses. Encourage self-assessments. Give opportunities to lead and succeed in games. Play games where winning and losing are matters of chance, rather than as a consequence of personal attributes. Emphasise this fact.

LYING/DENIAL OF RESPONSIBILITY

Behaviour	Assessment	Short-Term Management Strategies	Intervention Plans for Longer-Term Change
Problem Behaviour Lying/denial of responsibility. **Target Behaviour** Child will tell the truth and accept responsibility for her actions. **In order to do this the child needs to develop an 'internal locus of control' and feel that she can be effective.**	What does child deny? Does the child deny to everyone? Can the child accept making mistakes in any context? Can the child accept praise for positive behaviour/work? Is the child fearful of punishment? Is she unable to back down, fearful of losing face or self-esteem? *Competencies	Do not engage in arguments, especially in front of an audience. *Tactically ignore *Partial agreement: 'Maybe you didn't spill the paint, but I want you to help clear it up – we are all responsible for keeping the classroom tidy.' This also emphasises school ethos/values/rules. Consider the language used – avoid humiliation. Beware of labelling, e.g. 'liar'.	Raise awareness that we all make decisions and choices all the time and what is involved in this. Teach students the value of taking responsibility for the choices they make, emphasise this as part of 'growing up'. Give the child regular opportunities to make positive choices. Give positive feedback in terms of her progress towards self-responsibility. Praise honesty. Develop ethos where making mistakes are accepted as part of the learning process. Adults will need to model this. Model 'owning up'. Ask children what is the worst thing that could happen if they owned up. Use hypothetical situations to promote discussion. Develop cooperative, non-competitive ethos as much as possible.

Part Five: Emotional Distress

Children who are in emotional distress often behave in ways that are difficult to understand and manage.

Although individuals differ in their reactions to life events and there is rarely a simple cause and effect to children's distress, there are often precipitating factors. The more common of these are:

- unmet basic emotional needs for security, acceptance and warmth;
- the loss of a significant person without opportunities to grieve;
- physical and/or sexual abuse;
- witnessing violence and/or exposure to other trauma.

The way children behave is part of their struggle to come to terms with what has happened to them. Although the behaviour may not make sense to others it will fit in with the child's understanding and experience of the world. Teachers' reactions to that struggle can modify or exacerbate the distress. Acceptance of a child's feelings together with a gentle emotional response in a highly charged situation can often be useful and help to calm the child.

In practical terms and particularly in the context of a busy classroom, we always need to draw a balance between supporting the child who is distressed and containing the destabilising effect of his behaviour on the rest of the class.

In attempting to maintain this balance, educators need to acknowledge where their own sympathies, values and tolerance levels lie. There may be specific types of behaviour that trigger strong responses in some people. Not everyone finds the same behaviours irritating, upsetting or infuriating and it is important for individuals to be aware of what may lie behind their own responses.

There is a strong interactive factor in managing any aberrant behaviour. 'Strategies' do not exist in a vacuum outside of positive, well-developed relationships. It is worth noting that the word 'strategy' can be defined as 'the art of war' – not, perhaps, the most constructive basis for managing classroom relationships!

The following section offers a range of skills, interventions and management principles, related to specific examples of distressed and distressing behaviour. These are approaches which experienced practitioners have found useful. Some children experiencing emotional distress may eventually need more intensive intervention and individual support from a counsellor, psychologist or other support person. The ideas given here will support the child on an everyday basis before and when this occurs.

In attempting to deploy these various approaches, staff should identify their own training and support needs. Staying calm in a crisis is easy to say and less easy to do. Experience and training helps – as does a strong supportive network within the school.

* Starred suggestions in the following tables are explained in the Introduction.

UNPROVOKED AGGRESSION

Behaviour	Assessment	Short-Term Management Strategies	Intervention Plans for Longer-Term Change
Problem Behaviour Unprovoked aggression. **Target Behaviour** To express feelings without physical or verbal attacks on others. **In order to do this the child needs to raise awareness of the links between feeling, impulse and action and to increase awareness of the needs of others.**	*Context Where, when and with whom? *ABC to check that the incidents are unprovoked. *Frequency *Triggers *Onset Are there recent changes at home/school? *Perception Do other children link the aggression to rejection? Is there a need for social intervention?	Acknowledge feelings, but give a clear message of unacceptability about this behaviour within framework of mutuality, e.g. 'We do not hurt each other in this class. You are not allowed to hurt . . . No-one here is allowed to hurt you.' Give attention to the injured party. *Time-out Making the child say sorry is not often helpful. It can be a meaningless gesture. Later, the student may be expected to make reparations to the person he hurt (perhaps under adult supervision). *Consequences as choice	Develop child's ability to recognise his own feelings and to look for ways in which he can identify physical signs and take action based on thought rather than impulse. Discuss with the child: 1) the immediate consequences of his behaviour; 2) the longer-term consequences: relate these to the child's goals, e.g. to have friends. Teach other pupils to be *assertive. Catch the child being good – acknowledge all instances of self-control under difficult circumstances. *Circle of friends/peer support. Set up behaviour charts and rewards for agreed targets. Provide opportunities for child to express feelings safely, e.g. art activities, and to talk through anxieties. Involve parents closely, but sensitively, so that they do not feel blamed/threatened/ashamed.

OUT OF CONTROL TANTRUMS

Behaviour	Assessment	Short-Term Management Strategies	Intervention Plans for Longer-Term Change
Problem Behaviour Frequent 'out of control' tantrums. **Target Behaviours** 1) acceptable ways of expressing feelings; 2) ways of coping with frustration. **In order to do this the child will need to *recognise* what upsets her and take preventative action. The child may also need to feel more secure/confident generally, and interventions will need to be in place to secure this.**	*Context *Time and place and with whom. *Triggers *Frequency *Duration Check: *onset and any family changes. What do the family do that helps to calm the child? *Perception	Acknowledge the child's distress. Use clear brief communication to the child and state expectations quietly. Don't ask for explanations when she is upset/angry. Model calmness and self-control and use reassuring/soothing phrases. Assess the situation and deal with immediate danger(s) if there are any. Ensure safety – move the student or remove the audience if necessary. Give verbal commentary of what you are doing and reassure the child. Use help if available or ask for help – discreetly and calmly: demonstrate to pupil that you are in control. Send a responsible child if necessary. Do not restrain a child without another adult present unless not doing so would clearly put the child or others at greater risk. All physical contact with pupils should be in line with legislation and guidance.	Staff need to be aware of what may be triggers for the student in order to take evasive action/give familiar, calming activities. In consultation with parents/carers ensure all staff know about the best way of handling the child. Discussion with parents/carers may identify any insecurities, and interventions should be planned *jointly* between home and school as much as possible. Teachers should also be aware of behaviours they find particularly difficult and plan both their responses and the support they need in advance. Work with the child to help her identify what it is that is upsetting to her – this may not be the reason that would seem initially to be obvious. Work with the child on other ways of self-expression – developing language skills, artwork, puppets, drama, pretend play, stories, etc. Discuss major incidents in school with children in a non-blaming way. Pupils have been helpful in some schools with suggesting support strategies. Make it clear that the discussion is not about punishment but about support.

Fifteen minutes 'pupil focus' meetings, held regularly, which all staff attend, can be effective in terms of new ideas and shared strategies. This is also helpful in supporting individual staff who are in the 'front line' of more extreme behaviours.

For teachers who have established a positive relationship with the child the following may be useful:

If a child will accept it, a light touch on the hand/shoulder may be calming.

For younger pupils, gentle holding/rocking may be soothing. However, for some pupils, any physical contact will be unwelcome.

Offer face-saving solutions to the child.

STRONG REACTIONS TO PERCEIVED SLIGHTS/CRITICISM

Behaviour	Assessment	Short-Term Management Strategies	Intervention Plans for Longer-Term Change
Problem Behaviour Strong, distressed reactions to perceived slights/criticism. ***Target Behaviour*** To respond more appropriately. **In order to do this the child needs to develop:** **1) a more positive self image;** **2) more positive perceptions/ expectations of others.**	Are there specific issues to which the child is especially sensitive? Is the child reacting to specific peers/adults? *Perception *Competencies	Acknowledge the child's feelings. Help the child to 're-frame' the incident by pointing out possible different perspectives/explanations. *Take Two Find an opportunity as soon as possible afterwards to give positive feedback to the child.	The child could be asked to talk about how she feels when . . . (unwanted behaviour) happens, with drawings to illustrate. Work with a small group to identify what they find most difficult and different ways of thinking about and managing this. Teacher models acceptance of constructive criticism – perhaps asking how she could have done something better. Give children opportunities to self-evaluate or evaluate in pairs on specific tasks. Give messages to the child and others to promote the child's positive self-image. Look for opportunities to give private, positive and specific feedback. Children could be asked three things they are pleased with each day and three things they could have done better. They may then be asked to think about what they could have done to improve each situation. Paired work on the above may also help children to learn that constructive criticism is not a personal insult.

DESTRUCTIVE BEHAVIOUR (OWN WORK)

Behaviour	Assessment	Short-Term Management Strategies	Intervention Plans for Longer-Term Change
Problem Behaviour Destructive behaviour (own work). **Target Behaviour** To try his best and feel a sense of achievement, without setting unrealistic expectations of himself. **In order to do this the child needs to learn to feel successful, value his work and have realistic standards.** **Child may also need to know the boundaries of a piece of work so that his anxieties are contained.**	*Onset When? Which work? Which teacher? Which emotions does this action represent – anger, frustration, or unhappiness? *Perception What may be contributing to the child's poor self-image?	Acknowledge feelings. Focus on a recent success. Identify one specific aspect of the work that was satisfactory, e.g. underlining of titles / care taken with colouring, and inform the student. Ask the child to identify one benchmark for success. Maintain low-key response which is non-confrontational. Allow pupil to make three attempts and to choose the 'best of three'. Clarify main purpose of task: • content • accuracy • presentation *Take two Relocate the child to a place where he is less likely to make unfavourable comparisons between himself and others	Promote a sense of self-worth in *Circle work. Match work with the child's ability, in small steps if necessary, so that the child experiences success. Link new learning to what the child can do already. Encourage child to focus on his own progress and his *Personal best, not comparing with others. Develop class ethos in which mistakes are valued as part of the learning process. Adults model acceptance of mistakes and constructive criticism. Give opportunities for success, e.g. word processing written work if handwriting is poor. Don't stress perfection but an acceptable level of work. Involve child in mounting / displaying the work that he identifies.

71

DESTRUCTIVE BEHAVIOUR (OTHER PEOPLE'S THINGS)

Behaviour	Assessment	Short-Term Management Strategies	Intervention Plans for Longer-Term Change
Problem Behaviour Destructive behaviour (other's work/objects) **Target Behaviour** Treats things belonging to others with respect and does not touch them without permission. **The child may need to learn to:** • express anger more appropriately; • establish boundaries for her own behaviour; • build more positive relationships with others.	*Context *ABC Is this specific work or particular children's work? Check on the social relationships between the children involved. Is the destructive behaviour more general? * Pattern Are there recent changes at home or at school? Is the child expressing distress in other ways?	Acknowledge feelings but give clear message of unacceptability. Give attention to the child whose work has been destroyed. Negotiate compensation between children concerned. What can be done to 'make it up' to the child whose work has been destroyed? Give both children some choice in this – but do not discuss this at the height of the conflict. *Consequences as choice *Time-out	Help the child to identify what is really upsetting her, e.g. 'What were you thinking about when you did that?' Talk about how to recognise the physical signs of increasing anger/frustration. Talk through consequences of actions, teach how to develop a 'thinking gap' before action – counting slowly to ten, breathing slowly, teach relaxation skills. *Traffic lights or a similar signal to the teacher to ask for help. Give opportunities to express feelings appropriately and safely. Drawings, puppets, pretend play, even thumping a cushion has been known to work. Give praise and positive feedback for work and improved behaviour. Focus on empathy in *Circle work. Whole-class discussions, 'What can we do if we have a problem?' Generate strategies from the class. Teach *Conflict resolution strategies using role-play.

EPISODES OF DISTRESS AND CRYING

Behaviour	Assessment	Short-Term Management Strategies	Intervention Plans for Longer-Term Change
Problem Behaviour Frequent episodes of distress and crying. **Target Behaviours** To display more control over outbursts. To talk/express needs to an adult, or to begin to develop some problem-solving strategies. **In order to do this the child may need to learn to feel safe, secure about himself and family and feel that he has been heard.**	* Context *Frequency *Duration *Triggers What have been successful calming measures used previously? What possible factors at home/school may be contributing?	Give *Permission to cry. Outburst may be over quicker when this happens. Suggest the child moves to a more private place if necessary. Acknowledge the child's reasons for upset – there may be no need to 'solve' the problems at this time. Give reassurance, calming responses such as soothing phrases but do not give a high level of attention which may reinforce the behaviour. Physical comfort – an arm/shoulder/hand held; take the lead from the child about what is helpful. Promote a return to normal, with peer support, as soon as upset diminishes. Offer child a familiar, calming activity, perhaps in a quiet corner with a friend. Be careful not to be seen by the child and others to encourage the distress by rewarding it.	Show the student he will be listened to when he needs to talk about concerns. Identify an appropriate adult and time for this. Younger children may find a 'comfort' or 'transition' object helpful – a soft toy or something that belongs to a carer. Longer-term intervention will rely on home, school links and support, and the needs of individual involved. Provide as much security and positive self-esteem as possible in school. Develop the language of emotions within the curriculum to help children articulate their feelings. *Circle time activities to create an atmosphere of empathy. Peer support *Externalise the problem *Problem-solving discussion

HIGH LEVEL OF ANXIETY

Behaviour	Assessment	Short-Term Management Strategies	Intervention Plans for Longer-Term Change
Problem Behaviour Child displays high levels of anxiety and/or constant need for reassurance. ***Target Behaviour*** To display greater confidence and independence. **To do this the child may need to understand her fears and learn to feel effective.**	*Context *Frequency *Patterns Is this unfocused anxiety or a specific concern? What does child feel more confident about – in what circumstances? Is there a match between the child's ability and teacher expectations? Are there recent changes at home, e.g. birth of new baby, marital discord? Is the child watching TV or videos which are alarming her? *Competencies	Build in routine and predictability. Give prior warning of changes in routine. Have clear expectations. Reassure but also focus the child on the positive where possible. Link new activities/situations to what is familiar. Where the anxiety is acute encourage the child to breathe very deeply to help calm her down. Hold her hands if this is acceptable and model this deep breathing with her.	Help child to overcome fears where possible/appropriate. Some children may be afraid of failing/being ridiculed by others. With the whole class, develop clarity between 'laughing with' others and 'laughing at' others. Where the child's fears are real – perhaps about something happening at home, ensure she knows that she can talk with someone about this and that people will not be judgemental. Seek further advice. People are sometimes simply upset for the 'unknown' and they can't pinpoint specifics – it's OK to not find out why. Give the child choices and positive feedback for being effective. Give opportunities and positive feedback for independence. Teach self-talk and affirmations so the child can reassure herself. *Externalise problems

BLANKNESS AND DISENGAGEMENT

Behaviour	Assessment	Short-Term Management Strategies	Intervention Plans for Longer-Term Change
Problem Behaviour Blankness and disengagement. The child expresses very little emotion, does not engage positively with others and only participates in a very peripheral way. *Target Behaviour* To engage actively and positively with others and within the class group. To express feelings appropriately. **In order to do this the child may need to feel safe.**	*Onset Does the child understand what is happening in the class? Check: medical records hearing language skills. Talk with parents / carers, past teachers, peers. Ascertain past and recent behaviour. What is known about possible changes at home? Does the child have positive interactions in any situation? Which and with whom? *Ability	Offer limited choice opportunities. Make sure expectations are clear. Do not put pressure on the pupil but consistent behaviour management principles apply.	Show consistent warmth towards the child. Smile and greet the student by name. Speak to the child normally without demanding a response. Structure social interaction activities and games. A supervised paired activity would be a good place to start. Encourage the child to show someone else what to do. Perhaps give the pupil a non-verbal role in activities / group tasks. Boost confidence, self-perceived efficacy, e.g. 'I was pleased to see that you . . .'. Offer 'creative activities' to express feelings, e.g. music, drawing, PE, role-play, writing, puppets. Let the child know that you are available to listen to him if there is anything he wants to say. Structure non-threatening opportunities such as where the child 'helps' the teacher during playtime, which may provide opportunities for the child to talk. Do not subject the child to pressure to do so; let him find his own time.

Part Six: Unusual or Highly Inappropriate Behaviour

All behaviours occur on a continuum from what is considered normal to what is extremely unusual. From time to time, school staff may become concerned when children exhibit those rarer behaviours, which if they occurred as an isolated incident would probably go unnoticed, but are significant in terms either of their frequency or of their severity and duration.

Behaviour is a consequence ofx many interacting factors and school staff will, from time to time, have to make judgements about what is 'usual'. The benchmark is the context. In any given circumstances, what do the majority of the children appear to be doing and what is it that makes a particular child stand out from the rest? The age and cognitive level of the child is crucial in determining whether the behaviour is outside the 'normal range'. For example, it would be quite usual for a five-year-old to be distressed when initially left at school by parents, but such anxiety in a ten-year-old would be worrying, particularly if it has just suddenly begun to happen. Similarly, many children will from time to time become unwell as a result of childhood illnesses, or as a result of having eaten something that has not agreed with them, but the child who vomits everyday just before lunchtime or soils regularly will become a focus of some concern.

Some of the behaviours may be indicative of abuse and raise Child Protection concerns, while others are indicative of severe disturbance or other special needs, such as autism, which have gone unaddressed. In all cases where behaviour is unusual or highly inappropriate very careful monitoring should be maintained and a written record kept. All school staff should know how and when to seek advice, in particular in relation to Child Protection concerns. They also need to know about other agencies such as the Education Psychology Service and what they can expect in terms of informal guidance about specific concerns and for consultation on a named child at School Action Plus.

NB: *This section is not intended as an alternative to seeking the advice of other professionals.*

Where behaviour needs to be viewed within the context of the Local Education Authority's Child Protection procedures this would normally mean an initial discussion with the designated person within the school with responsibility for

Child Protection. This may result in a referral to Social Services or the Education Welfare Service. Where teachers have such concerns and are talking with the child about her behaviour, great care should be taken not to ask 'leading questions'; these may invalidate any subsequent investigation by Social Services.

Class teachers obviously need to deal with the behaviours as and when they occur in school and the following guidelines are intended to support this work. Some of these behaviours may be particularly distressing to teachers and other adults. Individuals should be aware of how the behaviour exhibited by some pupils may affect them, and the impact this may have on their ability to deal objectively with the situation. Staff will also need to bear in mind that although they may not be able to control the behaviour of some children, they, as professionals, should be able to control how they respond to those children. The established network within the school, together with advice from other agencies, should be able to provide both guidance and support for what are often very stressful situations.

Unless there are exceptional circumstances, which may put the child at risk, close communication with parents/carers is particularly important. Great sensitivity is required if it appears that the child may be displaying a cluster of behaviours found on the autistic spectrum. Such a diagnosis needs to be made by a medical professional.

There are some children in schools today who have experienced traumatic events in their lives. Certain behaviours may be related to this.

It is essential that careful assessments of behaviour are made over time and both the child and family are supported. Jumping to conclusions can be damaging to relationships and lead to inappropriate responses. The interventions given here are intended to help teachers manage situations during investigations and until more specific advice is given.

* Starred suggestions in the following tables are explained in the Introduction.

OBSESSIVE BEHAVIOURS

Behaviour	Assessment	Short-Term Management Strategies	Intervention Plans for Longer-Term Change
Problem Behaviour Obsessive behaviour, e.g. aversion to 'messy' activities with continual washing. ***Target Behaviour*** To reduce obsessive behaviour where it is impeding learning. **Child may need to reduce anxiety.**	*Onset *Frequency *Duration *Context What effect does behaviour have on learning or relationships? Do parents have similar concerns? Are there additional behaviours causing concern? (See ritualistic behaviour.)	Don't label the student or his behaviour, e.g. babyish. Minimise the attention given by other pupils. Give minimal attention to the child concerned, but attend to any safety issues immediately. Trying to stop the behaviour *suddenly* may be counter-productive. A related but safer activity could be offered instead. If possible, remove the child from a stressful situation.	It is appropriate to seek advice from an outside agency, particularly if this is one of a cluster of behaviours. Talk with child (if appropriate) to raise awareness of the behaviour and support him in reducing the behaviour. Give reassurance as appropriate in situations that may be stressful for the child. Introduce changes to routine as gradually as possible, with extra preparation for the change with the child concerned. It may be possible to link a work activity to strong interests. Focus on and encourage alternative activities, or permit the favoured activity at certain times, rather than trying to eliminate it. *Problem-solving discussions with the child: • identify the difficulty; • brainstorm possible solutions; • choose one to try; • carry out, monitor and review.

SOILING AND SMEARING

Behaviour	Assessment	Short-Term Management Strategies	Intervention Plans for Longer-Term Change
Problem Behaviour Soiling (and smearing) **Target Behaviour** Child needs to demonstrate appropriate toiletting behaviour. **Child may need to learn to feel in control psychologically as well as physically.**	Check medical history. Does the child have a history of difficulty with toilet training? The age of the child is an important factor. *Context *Onset Are there other concerns? Does the child try to assert control in other ways?	Organise the clearing up of any mess calmly with minimum fuss. Encourage independence of older children. The responsibility for cleaning depends on the child's age and knowledge of the pupil and her circumstances. Having an adult to help her may also provide opportunities for quiet discussion of concerns. The child should not, however, feel pressurised. Divert attention from incident, send the child to an adult outside of the classroom and occupy the other children. Avoid embarrassing the child as much as possible – acknowledge that she may be experiencing difficult feelings. Consult the named person in school for Child Protection and Special Needs Coordinator if the situation happens repeatedly.	Establish clear toiletting routines. Make sure that there is toilet paper, and soap available. Keep a supply of clean underwear and ensure that the children know that this is available if needed. Give curriculum input on bodily functions, signals and health and hygiene. Work as closely with parents/carers as possible to develop a non-punitive approach. Give pupil choices and opportunities to effect change, take responsibility, assert control in safe situations. Give opportunities for talking/listening in a safe space – appoint mentor/assistant if appropriate. Ensure there is curriculum input on personal autonomy and keeping safe. (See next page.) Be aware of any labelling and/or verbal bullying by peers and take prompt preventative action. Seek advice from outside agencies.

SEXUALLY EXPLICIT BEHAVIOUR

Behaviour	Assessment	Short-Term Management Strategies	Intervention Plans for Longer-Term Change
Problem Behaviour Sexually explicit play/behaviour, including masturbation in public. *Target Behaviour* To reduce the incidence of such behaviours. **In order to do this the child needs to learn that some behaviours are unacceptable. Approaches will depend on whether the child is behaving this way for attention, has poor/inappropriate social boundaries or as a manifestation of child abuse.** **A main focus should be on ensuring safety for the child and others.**	*Frequency *Onset Consider the age/cognitive levels of the child. Is there a mis-match? What exactly is being done/said? Is the child merely repeating words/behaviour to shock or do they appear to have an unnatural level of understanding? Are parents aware/concerned about this behaviour? Detailed records/monitoring are essential. Is this part of a cluster of other behaviours? Beware jumping to conclusions – keep an open mind.	Don't show shock/horror. Don't attribute blame. Don't ask leading questions. Distract the child if possible, without drawing attention to what is being done. Use *Positive language to focus on what they should be doing. Consult with the person responsible for Child Protection in the school and follow the Child Protection procedures. Immediate referral needs to be made to the appropriate agency if the child makes a disclosure.	Joint decisions about contacting parents/carers/other agencies need to be made. Curriculum intervention at an age-appropriate level for all children on keeping safe/telling adults/saying 'no' when they feel uncomfortable about the behaviour of others. For older pupils, input into health education programme about appropriate behaviour in differing contexts.

SELF-HARM

Behaviour	Assessment	Short-Term Management Strategies	Intervention Plans for Longer-Term Change
Problem Behaviour Child engages in self-harm, e.g. injures self with sharp object. **Target Behaviour** Reduction of incidence. **In order to do this the child may need to learn to feel better about himself and to stay safe.**	*Onset *Patterns *Triggers *Context *Perceptions What exactly is the child doing which is harmful? *Competencies	Do not show shock/horror. Acknowledge any feelings of anxiety that the child may have. Minimise the occurrence of stressful situations. Do not make assumptions; the child may be experiencing a range of emotions about himself and/or others. Offer a familiar activity/comfort. Express concern and caring – empower the child to cease this behaviour himself, stop him yourself if necessary. Speak to the child quietly and calmly tell him what you are about to do, e.g. 'Scott, I am going to sit down by you and hold out my hand so that you can give me the knife.' Consult with the named person for Child Protection in the school.	Monitor the use of scissors or other objects which the child may use to inflict harm. Structure activities to raise a sense of self-worth. Provide the pupil with opportunities for making choices, being in control, taking responsibility. Give regular positive attention. Structure opportunities for the child to develop a trusting relationship with an adult in school. Refer to outside agencies for advice; implement any programmes that have been suggested. *Problem-solving discussion to decide what else could happen when the impulse to self-harm occurs?

RITUALISTIC, REPETITIVE BEHAVIOUR

Behaviour	Assessment	Short-Term Management Strategies	Intervention Plans for Longer-Term Change
Problem Behaviour Ritualistic, repetitive behaviour, e.g. lining things up in the same order, repeating the same short play sequence over and over again. **Target Behaviour** **Child needs to limit this where it is impeding learning and social interaction.** **There may be a need to reduce anxiety for the child.**	*Context *ABC Assess the range and extent of any other difficulties. Is this part of a cluster of other unusual behaviours?	Do not demand that the behaviour ceases. Offer alternative behaviours where possible. Reduce any possible causes of anxiety.	Build in predictability and order as much as possible during the day. Reduce anxiety by preparing the child for any changes in routine. Use visual symbols to represent the sequences of activities/the day. A range of rewards may be needed to reinforce wanted behaviour positively. Some children will respond to praise, others less so. Rather than attempt to eliminate the behaviour altogether, it may be possible to locate it at certain points/times in the day, possibly as a reward. Seek advice from outside agencies.

BLURRING OF BOUNDARY BETWEEN REALITY AND FANTASY

Behaviour	Assessment	Short-Term Management Strategies	Intervention Plans for Longer-Term Change
Problem Behaviour Blurring of boundaries between fantasy and reality, e.g. where the child tells stories and insists they are events which happened or where there appear to be long-term effects from a film or story. **Target Behaviour** The child demonstrates that she is aware of the difference between what is real and what is not. Young children often range in their thoughts and talk from what is imaginary to what is real. The older the child the more this behaviour raises concerns.	What objective evidence is there that this is a problem? What exactly is the child saying and doing? *Context *Onset Consider the child's developmental stage – is immaturity a factor in her ability to understand? Are there other behaviours which are of concern? Are parents/carers also concerned?	Keep an open mind. Identify when/where this behaviour may be dangerous and take action to ensure safety. You may need to reassure the child and be clear to her about what is imaginary. Do not dismiss what the child is saying but acknowledge her perceptions. Do not accuse the child of 'telling lies'. This behaviour may be rooted in a need for attention, a cry for help, a real fear, which cannot be articulated. It may be one way of making sense of something that is happening or has happened.	Talk to the class about differences between true stories and made-up stories. Show how stories could have different endings – when they are not real we can choose the endings. Focus, where possible, on the predictability of the child's world and what is real. Debrief children after any role-play or similar activity. If this behaviour continues, is impeding the child's learning in any way or is amongst a range of other concerns advice should be sought from an outside agency.

UNSAFE ATTENTION-SEEKING BEHAVIOUR

Behaviour	Assessment	Short-Term Management Strategies	Intervention Plans for Longer-Term Change
Problem Behaviour Unsafe attention-seeking behaviour, e.g. climbing, taking risks with personal safety. **Target Behaviour** The child demonstrates that he is aware of what is dangerous and behaves appropriately to take care of himself and others.	*Onset *Context *Frequency *ABC Identify the actual behaviour causing concern – within individual incidents how much was the child in control; what did he actually do to protect himself from harm? Does the child seek attention in many other ways? From whom?	Use *Positive language to focus on the desired behaviour. Minimise your reactions and stay as calm as possible. Minimise sense of audience where possible, to reduce attention for negative behaviour. *Consequences as choice Ensure the safety of the child concerned, as well as others. Offer face-saving solutions where possible.	Work with the child to foster a sense of self-reliance and self-esteem. Give clear messages to the child about his value in the class. Ensure that there are ways for him to regularly receive positive attention. Help children to develop strategies to think before they act. Empower them to make 'positive choices'. Work with individuals to help them identify 'triggers' for this behaviour, including feelings. Provide alternative ways of handling anxiety/stress. Structure joint problem-solving activities for similar hypothetical scenarios – *Circle work. Show the child that you care about what happens to him and express concerns for his safety.

INDIVIDUAL EDUCATION PLAN		Name: _____ Class: _____	Age: _____ Date: _____
Difficulties the child is experiencing:	Target aim(s) for next 6 weeks:	ACTION PLAN Who will do what? State plans which relate to individual, group or class intervention and parent/carer involvement	REVIEW Date: _____ To what extent was the Action Plan carried through?
Basic assessment information:	Baseline information against which success can be measured:		To what extent was the target achieved?
What does the child most need to learn?		When/how often will interventions take place? How will progress be monitored/recorded?	Future Plans: a) maintain same or amended IEP b) change IEP to more appropriate target c) no further action d) other:

References and Resources

Ajmal, Y. and Rees, I. (eds) (2001) *Solutions in Schools: Creative applications of solution-focused brief thinking.* London: BT Press.

Bowkett, S. (1999) *Self-Intelligence: A handbook for developing confidence, self-esteem and interpersonal skills.* Stafford: Network Educational Press.

Canter, L. (1992) *Assertive Discipline.* Santa Monica, CA: Lee Canter Associates.

Collins, M. (2001) *Circle Time for the Very Young.* Bristol: Lucky Duck Publishing.

Cornelius, H. and Faire, S. (1989) *Everyone Can Win: How to resolve conflict.* Roseville, NSW: Simon and Schuster.

Curry, M. and Bromfield, C. (1994) *Personal and Social Education for Primary Schools through Circle Time.* Tamworth: NASEN.

Davies, G. (ed.) *Six Years of Circle Time.* Cardiff: Advisory Service for Education.

Decker, S., Kirby, S., Greenwood, A. and Moore, D. (eds) (1999) *Taking Children Seriously: Applications of counselling and therapy in education.* London and New York: Cassell.

DfEE (1998) Circular 1/98. London: The Stationery Office.

DfES (2002) *Don't Suffer in Silence.* Resource pack for schools. London: The Stationery Office.

Faupel, A., Herrick, E. and Sharp, P. (1998) *Anger Management: A practical guide.* London: David Fulton Publishers.

Fogell, J. and Long, R. (1997) *Emotional and Behavioural Difficulties.* Tamworth: NASEN.

Fox, G. (2001) *Supporting Children with Behaviour Difficulties.* London: David Fulton Publishers.

Fransella, F. and Dalston, G. (1990) *Personal Construct Counselling in Action.* London: Sage Publications.

Gourley, P. (1999) *Teaching Self-Control in the Classroom: A cognitive-behavioural approach.* Bristol: Lucky Duck Publishing.

Hyson, M. (1994) *The Emotional Development of Young Children: Building an emotion-centred curriculum.* New York and London: Teachers College Press.

Lewkowicz, A.B. (1999) *Teaching Emotional Intelligence: Making informed choices.* Melbourne: Hawker Brownlow Education.

Long, R. and Fogell, J. (1999) *Supporting Pupils with Emotional Difficulties.* London: David Fulton Publishers.

Maines, B. and Robinson, G. (1992) *The No-Blame Approach.* Bristol: Lucky Duck Publishing.

Maines, B. and Robinson, G. (1998) *All for Alex: A circle of friends*. Bristol: Lucky Duck Publishing.

Moll, L.C. (ed.) (1990) *Vygotsky and Education: Instructional implications and applications of sociohistorical psychology*. Cambridge: Cambridge University Press.

Moore, C. and Rae, T. (2000) *Positive People: A self-esteem building course for young children*. Bristol: Lucky Duck Publishing.

Morgan, A. (2000) *What is Narrative Therapy? An easy-to-read introduction*. Adelaide: Dulwich Centre Publications.

Mosely, J. (1996a) *Turn Your School Around*. Cambridge: Learning Development Aids.

Mosely, J. (1996b) *Quality Circle Time in the Primary Classroom*. Cambridge: Learning Development Aids.

Mosely, J. (1998) *More Quality Circle Time*. Cambridge: Learning Development Aids.

Pincus, D. (1992) *Manners Matter: Activities to teach young people social skills*. California: Schaffer Publishers.

Plummer, D. (2001) *Helping Children Build Self-Esteem*. London: Jessica Kingsley.

QCA (2000) *Curriculum Guidance for the Foundation Stage*. Hayes, Middlesex: QCA.

Rae, T. (1998) *Dealing with Feeling*. Bristol: Lucky Duck Publishing.

Rae, T. (2000) *Purrfect Skills: A social and emotional programme for 5–8 year olds*. Bristol: Lucky Duck Publishing.

Robb, J. and Letts, H. (1999) *Creating Kids Who Can Concentrate: Proven strategies for beating ADD without drugs*. Rydalmere, NSW: Hodder and Stoughton.

Roffey, S. (ed.) (2002) *School Behaviour and Families: Frameworks for working together*. London: David Fulton Publishers.

Roffey, S. and O'Reirdan, T. (2001) *Young Children and Classroom Behaviour: Needs, perspectives and strategies*. London: David Fulton Publishers.

Roffey, S., Tarrant, T. and Majors, K. (1994) *Young Friends: Schools and friendship*. London: Cassell Education.

Rogers, B. (1996) *Behaviour Recovery*. London: Pitman.

Rogers, B. (1997) *Cracking the Hard Class: Strategies for managing the harder than average class*. London: Paul Chapman.

Rogers, B. (2000) *Classroom Behaviour*. London: Books Education.

Sharp, P. (2001) *Nurturing Emotional Literacy*. London: David Fulton Publishers.

Tattum, D. and Tattum, E. (2000) *Bullying: The early years*. University of Wales, Countering Bullying Unit.

Ward, B. and Associates (1996) *Good Grief: Exploring feelings of loss and death with under 11s*. London: Jessica Kingsley.

Warden, D. and Christie, D. (1997) *Teaching Social Behaviour*. London: David Fulton Publishers.

Webster-Stratton, C. (2000) *How to Promote Children's Social and Emotional Competence*. London and New York: Paul Chapman Publishing.

Whitehouse, E. and Pudney, W. (1996) *A Volcano in My Tummy: Helping children to handle anger*. BC, Canada: New Society Publishers.